AFTER TIANANMEN

Other Books by the Author

Tiananmen Square: The Making of a Protest
The Long Game: How the Chinese Negotiate with India

AFTER TIANANMEN

THE RISE OF CHINA

VIJAY GOKHALE

HarperCollins *Publishers* India

First published in India by HarperCollins *Publishers* 2022
4th Floor, Tower A, Building No. 10, Phase II, DLF Cyber City,
Gurugram – 122002
www.harpercollins.co.in

2 4 6 8 10 9 7 5 3 1

Copyright © Vijay Gokhale 2022

P-ISBN: 978-93-5629-304-5
E-ISBN: 978-93-5629-305-2

The views and opinions expressed in this book are the author's own and the facts are as reported by him, and the publishers are not in any way liable for the same.

Vijay Gokhale asserts the moral right
to be identified as the author of this work.

All rights reserved. No part of this publication may be reproduced, stored in a retrieval system, or transmitted, in any form or by any means, electronic, mechanical, photocopying, recording or otherwise, without the prior permission of the publishers.

Typeset in 11.5/15.4 Minion Pro at
Manipal Technologies Limited, Manipal

Printed and bound at
Thomson Press (India) Ltd.

To Jayant and Sonali

Contents

Preface ix

Prologue xi

The Principal Players xvii

1. Survival 1
2. Quest for Prosperity 21
3. Playing the West 48
4. Wooing the Rest 71
5. The Malacca Dilemma 87
6. The Party Means Business 112
7. Attempts at Modus Vivendi 141
8. Conclusions 165

Acknowledgements 179

Notes 181

Selected Bibliography ....

Index 207

About the Author 219

Preface

I LEFT CHINA IN 1991, TWO YEARS AFTER THE TIANANMEN INCIDENT, AND returned for my second stint at the Indian Embassy in Beijing on the day after Deng Xiaoping's death in February 1997. Although I had been away for less than six years, the impact of Deng's economic reforms was already palpable in Beijing as well as in other parts of China to which I subsequently travelled over the next three years. The Tiananmen Incident of 1989 was a closed chapter so far as the Communist Party of China was concerned. If there were any lingering effects globally these could scarcely be discerned from the manner in which China was being wooed by the rest of the world. Deng's demise was condoled by leading international statesmen. President Bill Clinton described him as an 'extraordinary figure on the world stage'.[1] Jacques Santer, president of the European Commission, hailed Deng as the person who 'has made a mark on the twentieth century (and) shall be remembered by the whole world well into the twenty-first.'[2] UN Secretary General Kofi Annan called him the primary architect of China's modernization. There were, of course, references in the foreign media to the Tiananmen Incident of 1989 but the rich encomiums to Deng testified to the respectable position that China had secured on the world stage less than one decade after 1989.

For the next twelve years, from 1997 until the end of 2009, I was to continuously experience China in different capacities. I spent nearly seven years between Beijing and Taipei, and five years on the China desk in New Delhi. I marvelled at how deftly the Chinese Communist Party leadership steered China on a steady course to economic development and growth while maintaining its firm grip on power. India was going through its economic transformation at the time, and comparisons were inevitable. I also discovered that many Indians appeared to have a superficial understanding of China's politics, economy and foreign policy between 1990 and 2012. I hope that this book serves two purposes. First, to paint a picture of what happened in China during the twenty years between Deng Xiaoping and Xi Jinping. Second, to spotlight that it was during this 'interregnum' (from 1992 until 2012) that China laid solid foundations of its subsequent rise as a major global power. It is only through a better understanding of how China handled the changes and dealt with the challenges during this period when it was reintegrating with the global community that we, Indians, will be able to develop a proper understanding of today's China.

Prologue

THE RISE OF CHINA IS, PERHAPS, THE MOST CONSEQUENTIAL development of the early twenty-first century. Thus, a proper understanding of contemporary China is no longer an academic matter. For an emerging nation like India which is geographically situated on China's periphery, understanding its rise has become a matter of national importance. A Western perspective of China may not fully serve the purpose of building awareness and understanding, and greater research and writings by Indians will help in filling the gaps in our understanding of China from the Indian perspective.

My first book, *Tiananmen Square: The Making of a Protest*, dealt with a defining incident in contemporary Chinese politics, situated in the larger context of the 1980s, after China emerged from the chaos of the Great Proletarian Cultural Revolution and returned to the more normal pattern of development and international behaviour. In this book, I tell the story of the two decades after the Tiananmen Incident of 1989, an important but less written-about period in contemporary China. These twenty years were book-ended by the collapse of global communism (1989–1991) after the end of the Cold War on the one side and the Global Financial Crisis (2008–2010) on the other side. China was not immune to these developments. In fact, they presented China with fundamental challenges and critical choices to make. This is the story of how some of those choices were made and of who made them, as well as the larger story of how China quietly made its way up the global hierarchy of world power to manifest itself after 2012 as the primary challenger to the United States for world leadership.

The book is not intended to be a detailed factual rendition of China at the turn of the twenty-first century. It is about highlighting some key facets of the China story and addressing some popular misconceptions. It is sometimes felt that after 1992, China was led by uncharismatic leaders who sailed out on the tide of reforms that Deng Xiaoping had let loose, and somehow muddled through the next two decades until Xi Jinping emerged to lead China to greatness. The stories in this book are intended to establish that it was precisely during these twenty years, before Xi became China's president, that China experimented with bold ideas, demonstrated strategic vision, and laid the foundations for the pursuit of global power. It is because of what happened in China between 1990 and 2010 that President Xi Jinping is able to launch his global initiatives and seek Chinese hegemony.

The end of global communism and the fall of the Soviet Union made the Chinese communist state appear, at least for a few years, as if it were under siege from the surrounding democracies. Besides, at home, the Communist Party of China also faced the prospects of a revival of leftism. Deng Xiaoping had officially retired and others were in charge. As Soviet hardliners struggled to rein in the collapsing Soviet Union, their Chinese counterparts

PROLOGUE

tried to steer China away from reform. The first chapter is the story of 'Survival', of how Deng Xiaoping returned to active politics and overcame one final political challenge to his vision for China through wisdom and patience, and finally through action. It put paid to the myth that reforms in China after 1989 were smooth sailing or inevitable. It is also a reminder that factional rivalry is part and parcel of politics inside the Communist Party of China, and that its apparent invisibility ought not to be confused with non-existence.

The second chapter sheds light on the winding road that China traversed during its economic transformation to becoming the world's second-largest economy, the largest exporter of merchandise and the largest recipient of foreign direct investment by 2010. By the end of this period, the world became so dependent on China that it also became the critical engine for growth during the Global Financial Crisis of 2008. This 'Quest for Prosperity' was not only about good economic policy. It was also about the politics of managing systemic changes in the economy without weakening the Party's grip on power or causing social instability inside China. The choices that China made involved taking risks and showing political will. During this period the leadership coped with entirely new situations such as the insatiable demand for resources to feed the industrial machine. It includes the fascinating story about how China's leaders manoeuvred their country into the World Trade Organization scarcely a decade after Western sanctions had been imposed, and how the Western world became willing handmaidens to China's rise without realizing its full implications.

The third and fourth chapters of the book titled 'Playing the West' and 'Wooing the Rest' deal with some of the ways and means adopted by the Communist Party to craft a successful foreign policy that returned China to full international respectability within a decade of the Tiananmen Incident. Deeply suspicious of the true intentions of the United States towards communist China after the fall of the Soviet Union in 1991, the third chapter is the story of how China's leaders kept their true feelings hidden for twenty years and humbled themselves before the West in order to secure key foreign policy goals. They created the impression that China might be willing to accept a subordinate position in a Western-led world order in return for securing vast amounts of foreign capital and high technology that benefitted its economy. It also created a legion of international supporters in the rest of the world who pleaded China's case in global organizations and with sceptical governments. The fourth chapter tries to identify how China was able to expand its footprint across the world and make significant inroads into almost all the West's clients and constituencies across the globe by 2010.

The growth in Chinese diplomatic influence during these twenty years was complemented by the expansion of its military power. It was from the late 1990s that China began working towards building a world-class maritime force. The fifth chapter uncovers the nuts and bolts behind China's surreptitious acquisition of its first aircraft carrier. It looks at how and why President Hu Jintao posed the 'Malacca Dilemma' and began to look for remedies to secure the sea lanes of communication. The initial emergence of the QUAD at the end of the first decade of the twenty-first century also posed a diplomatic and potential military challenge to China. The Communist Party leadership had to address such external challenges while simultaneously revamping civil–military relations in the post-Deng era, since the new leaders of China lacked direct military experience and had to find a new modus vivendi with the People's Liberation Army in order to ensure the Party's control over the gun.

The Communist Party's evolution from 1990 to 2010 forms the core of the sixth chapter of the book, titled 'The Party Means Business'. As China became more internationally connected, the world wondered what would come after Tiananmen. The outside world became fascinated by the rise of the Princelings, the scheming ways of the Shanghai Faction and the army's business dealings, but post-Deng political arrangements held firm and China settled in for a period of political calm on the surface. Underneath, however, the steady erosion of ideology as the sociopolitical glue of the regime, and its replacement, almost insidiously, by a more potent and populist force of nationalism, with which the Party sought to bind the people to itself, went unnoticed by many. This chapter tells the story of how the Party adapted to changes in the post-Cold War period and how it internally evolved from being the representative of the working classes to becoming the primary backer of state capitalism. It is also the story of how corruption, in the short-term, led to booming economic growth, and of how the nexus between absolute power and massive corruption eventually became a serious problem for the Party.

The seventh chapter explores how India and China dealt with each other during the period when both were 'rising' in Asia while trying to find their place in a post-Cold War world. Beginning with Rajiv Gandhi's historic visit to China in December 1988, 'Attempt at a Modus Vivendi' traces the efforts on both sides to build common ground and discusses possible reasons as to why they failed to establish mutual trust.

The final chapter titled 'Conclusions' is a summation of the main themes in this book and is intended to tie this era in with the new Xi Jinping era. It seeks to explain how the successful economic reforms in China created a new set of challenges, what these meant for the future of the Chinese Communist Party and for China, and why Xi Jinping might have felt compelled to take some of the actions that he took early on in his first term after becoming the general secretary of the Party in November 2012.

This book is not, strictly speaking, a sequel to my earlier book *Tiananmen Square: The Making of a Protest*, but read together the two books trace developments in contemporary China from 1978 to 2012. I hope that this book will contribute to a better and more balanced understanding of how and why China has risen to be great power in this century.

The Principal Players

DENG XIAOPING: One of Mao Zedong's revolutionary comrades during the Chinese Revolution, Deng proved to be an able administrator for the newly established People's Republic of China. He was placed in key economic roles until the Cultural Revolution when, at Mao's behest, he was purged twice in 1966 and in 1976 but was spared from imprisonment and physical torture, possibly because of his unique managerial skills. After surviving the efforts of Mao's wife Jiang Qing and the Gang of Four to eliminate him, Deng emerged as China's tallest leader in 1978 and steered the country on the path to economic reform and international respectability. He overcame political setbacks due to the fall of his two main lieutenants – Hu Yaobang and Zhao Ziyang, survived the Tiananmen crisis of 1989 and finally retired from all offices at the end of 1989, though he was to remain China's most influential political figure until his death in February 1997. Deng is considered to be the core of the second generation of communist leadership.

THE PRINCIPAL PLAYERS

JIANG ZEMIN: Born in 1926 and educated at Shanghai's Jiaotong University, Jiang joined the Communist Party of China in 1946. He was able to escape the worst excesses of the Cultural Revolution while working in Wuhan, before rising through the electronics bureaucracy in the early 1980s. His appointment as the mayor of Shanghai in 1985 and his subsequent promotion as its party secretary in 1987, along with his nomination to the politburo, elevated him to the higher echelons of power. His nomination as the general secretary of the Chinese Communist Party in June 1989 after the Tiananmen Incident came as a total surprise. Defying predictions that he would be no more than a transitional figure, Jiang survived the political machinations of the Party Elders, outlived Deng and sidelined his rivals to become the face of China (as president) and of the Communist Party (as general secretary) through the 1990s. His buffoonish external persona concealed a shrewd and cunning mind that allowed him to exercise authority even after demitting all offices by 2004. He continues to wield influence in China until this day. Jiang is considered to be the core of the third generation of communist leadership.

ZHU RONGJI: Born in 1928 and educated in engineering at Qinghua University in Beijing, Zhu stood out due to his personal characteristics as an outspoken and no-nonsense individual. He was exiled twice during Mao's period for being excessively critical of his policies, but his undoubted competence as an administrator led to his successive appointments as mayor of Shanghai (1987), Shanghai's party secretary (1989), vice premier (1991), and premier of the People's Republic of China (1998–2003). Although he held the premier's position for just five years, Zhu left his imprimatur on every aspect of China's economy and can be regarded as the leader who did more than any other to fulfil Deng Xiaoping's vision of 'reform and opening up'.

HU JINTAO: Born in 1942, Hu studied engineering at Qinghua University. Growing up during the Cultural Revolution, during which he was exiled to Gansu province, Hu rose through the ranks of the Communist Youth League after 1982 before coming to Deng's notice when he was the party secretary for Tibet (1988–92). A surprise appointment to the Politburo Standing Committee in 1992 put him in pole position to succeed Jiang Zemin as China's top leader. In contrast to Jiang's cartoonish personality, Hu was bland and nondescript even as he rose to the highest offices of vice president of China (1998–2003), general secretary of the Party (2002–2012), president of China (2003–2013), and chairman of the Central Military Commission (2005–2013). He is regarded as the core of the fourth generation of leaders.

WEN JIABAO: Born in 1942, Wen like Hu studied at Qinghua University and joined the Chinese Communist Party just before the Cultural Revolution. He came to the attention of senior leadership when he was appointed as deputy director of the powerful General Office of the Party in 1985, promoted a year later to director, and served three general secretaries in that capacity until 1992. In many ways, Wen's political survival when he was so closely associated with Zhao Ziyang (even accompanying him to Tiananmen Square on 19 May 1989) is intriguing and has never been fully explained. He nonetheless survived the fall of his mentors and went on to become vice premier under Premier Zhu Rongji, whom he eventually succeeded in March 2003 until 2013. Adopting a meek demeanour, Wen tried to project himself as empathetic to the ordinary Chinese.

:CHAPTER 1:

Survival

NINETEEN EIGHTY-NINE WAS A DECISIVE YEAR FOR CONTEMPORARY China, and not merely because of the Tiananmen Incident. Aside from the internal political challenge to the Communist Party and the problems of an overheated economy, the very fate of global communism seemed to hang in the balance that year. For Deng Xiaoping, personally, the next two years would be filled with trials and tribulations, as he struggled to stabilize China and transfer power to the next generation of Chinese leaders. On the day after martial law was declared in Beijing (20 May), Deng was to characterize these challenges that 'our party and state faced [as] a life-and-death crisis.'[1] In more than one way, therefore, it was a question of survival.

There was one matter on which there was total unanimity within the top leadership – that they had emerged from a life-and-death struggle in the summer of 1989. This bolstered their conviction that the Party was supreme and that its absolute leadership had to be preserved at any cost. Deng led this camp of true believers. It is true that he had called for bringing political changes in the Party's style since the beginning of the 1980s, but only to the limited extent that it minimized the possibility of a cult of a Mao-like personality or another Cultural Revolution-like movement occurring again in the future. In his secret memoirs, published posthumously, Zhao Ziyang confirmed that Deng's ideas of political reform 'were precisely to consolidate the Communist Party's one-party rule. Deng firmly rejected any reform that would weaken that.'[2] Deng was especially critical of the multi-party system and the Western notions of parliamentary democracy.[3] (Xi Jinping has reiterated the same political line in Party Document No. 9 that was issued in 2013.) For that matter, even Zhao Ziyang had never conceived of a Western-style democracy in China. He would make this clear in his memoir. 'Of course, the political reform I had in mind for China at the time, up until 1989, was not an adaptation of a multi-party system. Nor did I think that the Communist Party's ruling position should change,' wrote Zhao. 'Our hope is for the ruling position of the Communist Party to be maintained for a considerable period.'[4] The West's hopes in Zhao Ziyang had been misplaced.

The immediate question at hand for the Chinese Communist Party, and Deng personally, was the selection of the new leadership. Beyond the consensus over Zhao Ziyang's ouster and the importance of selecting a new general secretary who had to be ideologically committed to defending the Party's absolute supremacy, the seven ageing men (Deng Xiaoping, Chen Yun, Li Xiannian, Yang Shangkun, Bo Yi Bo, Wang Zhen, Peng Zhen) and one ageing woman (Deng Yingchao) were divided on who that person should be. The conservative group among the Party Elders, led by Chen Yun, suggested names that Deng feared might take the Party in a leftward direction. Deng favoured Li Ruihuan, the mayor of Tianjin City, whom he saw as both energetic and as an effective economic manager, but he could not garner support for his candidate. Rather than engaging in another bruising fight, Deng decided to informally consult with the two leading conservatives – Chen Yun and Li Xiannian. The three of them were able to reach a consensus on two points. First, on personnel appointments, Deng accepted Chen Yun's choice of Jiang Zemin, the party secretary of Shanghai City, to replace Zhao Ziyang as the new general secretary of the Communist Party. This was despite the fact that Jiang Zemin did not have overtly reformist credentials. In return, Deng secured a seat on the Politburo Standing Committee for his candidate, Li Ruihuan. The new seven-member Politburo Standing Committee – comprising Jiang Zemin, Li Peng, Qiao Shi, Yao Yilin, Li Ruihuan, Song Ping – finalized at Deng's residence on 27 May 1989, represented an untidy compromise. Though not entirely to Deng's liking, it kept the balance and helped stabilize the political situation quickly. Second, on the policy front, Deng secured an assurance from the conservatives – Chen Yun and Li Xiannian – that this new leadership team would be politically committed to Deng's policy of economic reform and opening up.[5] Economic reform was, for Deng, the most important legacy that he wished to leave behind, and he was prepared to make the deal with his rivals over personnel choices if it meant that his policies would not be derailed. This showed, once again, Deng's capacity for compromise in order to advance long-term strategic objectives.

Deng used the compromise that he had worked out with Chen and Li to curb the authority of Premier Li Peng and Vice Premier Yao Yilin, whom he saw as trying to thwart the economic reforms in 1987–88. He shrewdly circulated a document containing the details of the compromise to the entire Party's top leadership. In this document, Deng referred to the consensus that had been reached by the Party's senior leaders on the continued relevance and importance of the policies, in order to publicly nail down the deal that the troika had privately reached. His message to the Party was clear: 'The policies of reform and opening up to the outside world should remain unchanged for dozens of years.'[6] Deng chose his first public appearance after suppressing the Tiananmen protest to deliver this clear message to the people of China as well, and to the world at large. Addressing the senior military leaders on 9 June 1989, he said China would invest heavily in the basic industry even if it meant temporarily going into debt; it would take more financial risk through borrowings; and it would focus on infrastructure.[7] In subsequent talks he argued for joint ventures created with foreign capital, supported special development zones with a robust foreign presence and called on the new leadership to demonstrate through policy actions that there would be no change in China's policy of opening up. In one meeting, he even went so far as to praise the fallen General Secretary Zhao Ziyang for his bold economic policies despite the grave political mistakes that had been committed by him.[8] In this way he ensured that attempts by those who held the administrative reins, especially Premier Li Peng, would not be able to sabotage the reform process.

Even as China's leadership was grappling with political succession and economic reforms, it was compelled to turn its attention to the happenings abroad, especially inside Eastern Europe.[9] Developments in Poland were of particular concern in mid-1989. Solidarity, the independent trade union led by Lech Walesa, that had pressured the Polish state to hold an election, won on the very day that Chinese tanks had rolled into Tiananmen Square (4 June). Hungary was another source of worry. The mortal remains of Imre Nagy, a former communist hero who had led the anti-communist revolt in 1956 and paid with his life, was honourably reburied in the presence of thousands of Hungarians in a show of defiance to the communist rulers of Hungary (16 June). Neither of these developments had any significant impact on the protests happening inside China, but as the anti-communist movements in Eastern Europe snowballed through the late summer and early autumn of 1989, the Chinese grew anxious. Soviet President Mikhail Gorbachev's criticism about the use of military force by the Chinese Communist Party to suppress the Tiananmen Square movement, in his speech to the Supreme Soviet on 1 August 1989, would have exacerbated these anxieties since the Communist Party of the Soviet Union was regarded as the vanguard of international communism.[10] Deng tried to stem such anxieties in a talk with the leading members of the Central Committee in September 1989. 'I think the upheavals in Eastern Europe and the Soviet Union were inevitable,' he said. 'It is hard to predict how far they will go; we shall have to observe developments calmly.'[11] He urged them to study the situation carefully before reacting to it. The Chinese Communist Party began a detailed examination of the reasons for the breakdown of communism in Eastern Europe, with the purpose of learning the right lessons in order to avoid sharing the fate that had befallen their European comrades. Special study groups were set up by the Chinese Academy of Social Sciences to study the collapse of communism. This project was later deemed to be of such importance that it was designated as a fundamental national social science research topic.[12]

One fallout of this development was the prolongation of the Zhao Ziyang case. (He had been dismissed as the Party's general secretary in May 1989 but the leadership had to still determine how to politically and legally deal with him.) The Party had initially hoped to resolve his case by the end of 1990 after the Special Investigation Group had submitted their report, on his culpability in allowing the political disturbances in May 1989, to the Central Committee. The idea was to move on. However, developments in Eastern Europe appeared to cause the Party to rethink their approach towards Zhao. The Party grew concerned that he might become a rallying point for the anti-communist forces both domestically and internationally if their actions made an apparent martyr of him. They wanted to assess how he thought about what was happening in Eastern Europe. Zhao Ziyang recounts how, in February 1990, the Head of the Special Investigative Unit, Wang Renzhong, unexpectedly shared a batch of documents with Zhao relating to the events in Eastern Europe and asked him to expound his views on the drastic changes taking place in Europe.[13] They were trying to gauge his thoughts on the matter due to their concerns that he might become a magnet for the anti-regime sentiment. His case eventually dragged on until the end of 1992. Even after his case was settled, he remained under house arrest for many years. His rare visits outside were closely supervised.

Once the internal political situation had stabilized and the economic policy had been steered back onto the reform track, the Party grappled with the question of how the student demonstrations had garnered so much support. The Party suspected the Western 'hand'. On 1 June 1989, the Ministry of State Security sent a report to the politburo claiming that the Americans wanted to subvert socialism in China, and that after Hu Yaobang's demise this 'has taken the form of direct intervention and open support for the turmoil.'[14] Western media reportage as well as the response of Western governments to the Tiananmen 'massacre' hardened these suspicions enough for Deng to tell Chinese-American Nobel laureate Prof. Tsung-Dao Lee, in September 1989, that the West was 'waging a world war (*against socialism*) without gun smoke'.¹⁵ A similar allegation was reiterated when Deng received former Tanzanian President Julius Nyerere in Beijing in November 1989.¹⁶ An internal document that was believed to contain comments attributable to Deng, that circulated within the Party in early 1990, warned Party members that the West would spare no efforts to topple the communist regime.¹⁷ The fall of the Berlin Wall (9 November), the subsequent collapse of communism throughout Eastern Europe in 1989–90, and the end of the Soviet Empire in August 1991 would all add further layers of certainty to the Party's belief that China would be the next American target. The seeds for the rivalry between China and the United States that would sprout after Xi Jinping assumed the presidency in 2013 were, in reality, already sown in the aftermath of the Tiananmen crisis. In this sense, the Tiananmen Incident in 1989 is a fundamental turning point in both China's domestic and foreign policies.

As the year 1989 moved towards a close, Deng prepared to demit all the formal trappings of power. He had already hinted at this prospect when, on 16 June 1989, while addressing the new leadership line-up, he had declared his intention to step down from all his responsibilities. 'I'll get out of everybody's way,' is what he was reported to have said.¹⁸ Therefore, he handed over the last formal position – the chairmanship of the Central Military Commission – to General Secretary Jiang Zemin in November 1989. He felt that this might be the only way to compel the other Elders to leave active politics and end their interference in the reform and opening up of China. He bet on the fact that he would still wield adequate behind-the-curtains influence despite being plain Comrade Xiaoping, but an unanticipated series of international developments would again delay his full retirement from politics. First, European communist regimes collapsed faster than anyone had envisaged. Second, the

Communist Party of the Soviet Union (CPSU) showed signs of terminal decline. The latter was of greater concern to the Chinese communists because Soviet communism was their polar star. The survival of the CPSU was thought important for the CCP in both an ideological way because they were fraternal parties and from the perspective of national security because China did not want Russia to gravitate into the Western camp.

The infighting that had erupted within the CPSU led to the consolidation of a hard-line anti-Gorbachev faction that was ideologically committed to reversing his policies of 'glasnost' (political reform) and 'perestroika' (economic reform). They blamed Gorbachev's misplaced policies as the cause for the collapse of Soviet communism. The Chinese did so too. Deng, however, was far more concerned about the anti-reform faction in the CPSU making common cause with hardliners inside the Chinese Communist Party to target his reforms in China. Deng faced a dilemma. He could not allow the Soviet Communist Party to collapse, and he did what he could to prop it up by quietly lending it support. On the other hand, the ascendancy of the anti-reform hardliners in the CPSU would encourage the 'left' in China to block Deng's economic reforms. This dilemma would present Deng with the final political challenge of his career.

Deng tried to nip the problem in the bud in December 1989 by circulating a document to 'unify thinking' within the Party on the developments in Europe. His main argument was that communism had collapsed not because of political or ideological weaknesses in European communist parties but because they had failed to deal with economic problems.[19] In March 1990, he again urged the leading members of the Central Committee to steadily develop relations with the Soviet Union without publicly arguing about ideological differences.[20] He wanted to prevent debate over the collapse of communism from taking an ideological hue. The Party's focus had to stay on reforms. He realized that he was fighting an uphill battle. Deng's worst fears were soon realized. A neo-leftist group within the CCP claimed that the imminent danger to the Party came from 'ideological contamination'.[21] The problem with the Soviet Union was caused, they claimed, by Gorbachev's 'revisionist' policies (he had turned his back on communist doctrine and practice with his policies of glasnost and perestroika). The spearhead of the attack against Deng was his namesake, Deng Liqun, a conservative ideologue who had been sidelined in 1987 for his doctrinaire opposition to the reforms. 'Little' Deng (as he was known) had regained influence after 1989 with the backing of Elders Chen Yun and Wang Zhen, and was also being encouraged in his efforts to stall the reforms by the 'planning faction' in the Politburo Standing Committee – Premier Li Peng, Vice Premier Yao Yilin, and Song Ping. The opponents to Deng's reforms also had substantial influence inside the Party's organization and propaganda departments, which allowed them to spread the message to the rank and file of the CCP. Although Deng had a deal with his rivals on continuing with economic reforms, it was threatening to fall apart because the collapse of communism in Eastern Europe seemed to provide fresh encouragement to the hardliners inside the Party.

This teaming up of Deng's political rivals and the left ideologues in 1990 marked a particularly dangerous phase in China's journey to modernization. Deng was not wrong in assuming that their real target was his policies of reform and opening up. He was fighting hard to keep China on the road to economic reform. In January 1990, Deng holidayed in Shanghai. This was not a coincidence. According to Deng's biographer, Ezra Vogel, he had decided that this city would spearhead his next major reform effort. Its geographical location (the Yangtze or the Chang Jiang river delta), its history as a trading hub in the first half of the twentieth century and its reform-minded leadership (Deng was taken up with Zhu Rongji, the new party secretary of Shanghai for his commitment to economic reform and his leadership qualities) offered a perfect combination to experiment with reforms in Shanghai.[22] When he returned to the national capital, Deng urged the new Politburo Standing Committee to focus on Shanghai. His advice seemed to fall on deaf ears. In March 1990, he publicly articulated his concern that if the annual rate of growth remained at 4 to 5 per cent, it would represent a decline in the Chinese economy relative to the global economy. He again urged the Central Committee to seize this opportunity to develop the economy and declared that both the planned economy and the market economy were necessary for China to develop. 'Don't be afraid of taking a few risks,' he urged his colleagues.[23] Realizing the importance of keeping the West engaged with China, Deng also continually messaged Western leadership during the same period. In October 1989, he told former US President Richard Nixon that China would be happy to have American merchants continue doing business with China, and this was reiterated when he met with former Canadian Prime Minister Pierre Trudeau in July 1990. 'Despite the trouble that has arisen in Eastern Europe and the Soviet Union,' he told Trudeau, 'and despite the sanctions imposed by seven Western countries (G-7), we adhere to one principle: to maintain contacts and build good relations with the Soviet Union, United States and also with Japan and European countries. We have never wavered in this principle.'[24] But through the summer of 1990, Deng appeared to be losing power to his rivals. At the Seventh Plenary Meeting of the Thirteenth Central Committee in December 1990, a fierce debate brought the divide out into the open. Chen Yun and Deng Liqun, among others, declared that market-oriented reforms would lead to the restoration of capitalism in China, and the 'peaceful evolution', which the West wanted in order to bring about the demise of Chinese socialism.

That year, Deng's principal rival for power, Chen Yun, also opened a new front against him over the issue of corruption. It was a fact that corruption was growing inside the Party and the government after the reforms were introduced in the early 1980s. Family members of prominent revolutionaries and their cronies saw new opportunities to enrich themselves, as China opened up and foreign money flowed in. Who better to navigate the complex underworld of Chinese politics than the children and grandchildren of China's leading cadres? In time, they would come to be known as '*tai zi*' (princelings). A strong nexus was developing between this group of 'influencers' and Western investors, and even foreign governments. General Secretaries Hu Yaobang (1980–87) and Zhao Ziyang (1987–89) had irked the conservative leadership by trying to curb the malaise. Now the opposition saw an opportunity to use it to target Deng by placing on his shoulders the responsibility of allowing corruption to flourish as a result of economic liberalization. Chen Yun declared that the Western liberal ideas that had entered China, as a consequence of the policies followed by Hu Yaobang and Zhao Ziyang, were the primary reason for the spread of corruption, and hinted that Deng had to share some of this blame.[25] Chen Yun's assault on Deng emboldened people like Premier Li Peng and Vice Premier Yao Yilin to re-emphasize the role of central planning and to talk of balanced growth, which contradicted Deng's call for China to move to very high growth rates in order to catch up with the West. Despite the political assaults on him, Deng made yet another attempt in January 1991 to regain momentum for his reforms when he paid a return visit to Shanghai and publicly said that he regretted not including Shanghai in the original list of special economic zones, with which China had begun experimenting with the market economy in the early 1980s. Deng's comments on this occasion did not even merit a mention in the official media. By then, the grip that 'Little' Deng (Deng Liqun) and left-leaning ideologues had on the Party's propaganda machine was so all-pervasive that even Deng Xiaoping found it hard to deliver his message to the Chinese people. Deng was eventually forced to resort to subterfuge to sneak his ideas into the national daily. He wrote under the pseudonym 'Huangfu Ping' in the *Liberation Daily*, which belonged to Shanghai City and was under Zhu Rongji's control.

By mid-1991, it seemed as if Deng was slipping away into political oblivion. China's tryst with reform stood at a vital political crossroads, with the green light indicating a turn towards the left. The new general secretary, Jiang Zemin, also felt that the political wind was changing direction. After his return from an official visit to Moscow in May 1991, he made a speech on the anniversary of the Party's founding (1 July), in which Maoist ideas of class struggle against 'bourgeois' liberalism, and the accusation that Western forces hostile to China were working to topple communism, made a reappearance. Just when it seemed that China would turn to the 'left' again, the developments in the Soviet Union worked in Deng's favour. A coup d'état by anti-Gorbachev hardliners on 19 August 1991 was foiled by Boris Yeltsin in Moscow and Anatoly Sobchak in Leningrad (St Petersburg). The initial news of the events in the Soviet Union was welcomed by the conservatives in the Chinese Communist Party. A document reportedly made the rounds calling it a victory for Chinese communism as well.[26] There was talk about how the coup leaders had successfully foiled a Western plot to subvert

Soviet communism. Deng, who still wielded some influence, called a meeting at his residence the very same day and urged others to refrain from publicly commenting on the situation. He was worried about the West's reaction to the statements of Chinese support for the coup leaders. The economic reforms and double-digit growth rates that he had planned for China would not be possible without Western financing, trade and technology. He, therefore, urged his colleagues not to air their views about how the West had created troubles for the Soviet Union as well as for China. 'We should not repeatedly mention the peaceful evolution plot by the West,' he is reported to have said, 'we need the United States to promote our reform and opening up. If we confront the US, we will leave ourselves with no room to manoeuvre.'[27] Fortunately for Deng, by 21 August 1991 the abortive coup in Moscow had failed. This was the opportunity that he was waiting for to reassert his influence. The reformists began to claw their way back with his support. One of their first acts was to bring the reformist-minded Zhu Rongji, the party secretary of Shanghai, to Beijing as vice premier and give him the responsibility of dealing with economic issues. With him in a key economic post, the reformists gained in strength. They subtly began to reshape public narrative about the causes for the collapse of communism in the Soviet Union. Instead of blaming the West outright, the reformists spoke about the economic mistakes made by Gorbachev, and the negative consequences of ill-advised political reforms that he had experimented with. For the next several months, until the end of 1991, the policy debate over reforms sharpened. Both camps engaged in proxy battles through the media. During this time, Deng rarely took issue with others publicly, preferring to let his proxies speak on his behalf. The propaganda machinery continued to remain in the hands of Deng Liqun and other 'leftist' forces, and that was a problem for Deng. Chen Yun's son, Chen Yuan, co-authored an article in September 1991 that criticized romantic notions of capitalism and economic reforms, and highlighted that the real problem came from the liberal political thinking that was being encouraged as a result. Deng counter-attacked through Yang Shangkun who, in October, declared that the threat of Western subversion should not be overemphasized.[28] In November, one of the most conservative senior leaders, Wang Zhen apparently flew into a rage and hinted that Deng was going down the capitalist road.[29] The proverbial last straw for Deng was the attempt by left-leaning veterans to criticize the special economic zones, the jewel in Deng's crown, as a 'capitalist' experiment and as a 'breeding ground for Western political ideas and thinking'.[30] Deng had finally had enough.

Although Deng had officially been in 'retirement' since November 1989, he deemed it necessary to re-emerge in public to personally wage this particular battle. Too much was at stake here. In January 1992, Deng took all seventeen members of his family on a railway train to holiday once again in southern China. Apparently, he notified nobody in the Party about his departure. According to various accounts, his purported vacation was arranged in secret through the People's Liberation Army (PLA). Deng could still trust this constituency. He had strong pre-revolutionary ties to the PLA that he had nurtured throughout his subsequent political career. He journeyed by train to visit the places which were sites of China's early economic success stories – Shenzhen, Zhuhai and Shanghai. These visits were not reported in the media, but Deng made very certain of showing himself in public wherever he went. He visited special economic zones, factories, bridges and markets. He touted the benefits of economic reform and criticized its opponents. And as the saying goes, a rolling stone gathers momentum. Even though the official propaganda machinery was discouraged from covering his tour, and Deng himself held no press conferences, dozens of reporters from Hong Kong descended on Guangdong province where he was visiting and documented the growing public support that he was garnering. Once the Hong Kong media had broken the story, the officials in Beijing were confronted with a difficult choice: either to ignore Deng's trip to the south or acknowledge it, which might embarrass them. The latter would also have meant tacitly acknowledging the weakness in their position.[31] Hence the official media chose the option of continued radio silence. Deng expected this to happen. He was focused on mobilizing support for his economic reforms from among local leadership in the south (this region of China was the major beneficiary of reforms in the 1980s). Being the beneficiary of ten years of reform, the provincial leadership lined up behind Deng one after another, accompanying him everywhere during his tour, and finally, forcing the top leadership in Beijing to sit up and take notice.

In several informal talks during this tour, Deng delivered crucial messages that were to form the building blocks of his subsequent assault on the opposition at the centre. First, Deng proclaimed that China had weathered the storm of Tiananmen because of the economic reforms, thus signalling that economic liberalization was not the cause of the political storm that had hit China in 1989. Second, he compared making reforms by emancipating the forces of production with revolution. By equating reform with revolution, he blunted any possibility of the 'left' accusing him of permitting counter-revolutionary activity. Third, Deng rejected the main argument of the leftists that reform would allow back-door entry to Western capitalism through the establishment of foreign-invested joint ventures within China. He said that this could not happen because foreign enterprises operated under Chinese law and policies. Fourth, he declared development to be the supreme principle. 'Like a boat sailing against the current, we must forge ahead or be swept downstream,' he said. And he urged people to take risks and to courageously experiment. 'We must not act like women with bound feet,' was his advice to the local officials.*

His final point was to hammer the first nail in the leftists' 'coffin' by declaring that 'at present we are being affected by both "Right" and "Left" tendencies. But it is the "Left" tendencies,' he said, 'that have the deepest roots. Some theorists and politicians try to intimidate people by pinning political labels on them. That is not a Right tactic but a Left one.' Deng drew a direct connection between this 'Left tendency' and their argument that the reform-and-opening-up policies were a means of introducing capitalism and eroding socialism in China, allowing him to label the left-wing of the Party as anti-reform and anti-people.[32] It was during what came to be known as his 'southern tour' (*nan xun*) that the tide finally began to turn in Deng's favour.

Throughout the southern tour, the leadership in Beijing had still not categorically spoken out in his support. Both sides of the divide used high-level proxies in an attack–counterattack mode. Deng decided to enlist the support of the PLA. Although he had given up his official position as the chairman of the Central Military Commission, he still had dominating influence

---

* The Chinese practice of binding the feet of women in China, in order to deform and hamper their natural walk as adults, was widely practised in the Chinese Empire, and was only discontinued in the twentieth century.

on the PLA, and it was to them that he turned in this hour of need. He asked President Yang Shangkun (first vice chairman of the Central Military Commission) and his half-brother General Yang Baibing (PLA's chief political commissar) to demonstrate their support for his mission by endorsing the importance and necessity for the economic reform and opening up of China. The Yang brothers did so. General Yang Baibing even went as far as to declare that the PLA would serve as 'protector and escort' of the reform process.[33] Some labelled the PLA as 'the armed escort of reform'.[34] Those in the national capital, Beijing, understood that power was shifting in favour of Deng and, consequently, General Secretary Jiang Zemin started to align himself with Deng's position. In March 1992, a month after he had completed his southern tour, Deng felt adequately emboldened to circulate the gist of his talks on the tour in the form of a Party document (Document No. 2). It was circulated in the politburo, and ultimately approved by it. Vice Premier Zhu Rongji was invested as the executive Vice Premier with overall responsibility for the economy. The blanket of silence that the leftist ideologues had been able to impose over Deng for nearly eighteen months began to tear. Finally, on 31 March 1992, the *People's Daily* published the first detailed account of Deng's trip to the south under the title 'East Wind Brings Spring All Around'. Once the media dam was breached, Deng's southern tour gained wide publicity in China. It has since come to be known to every Chinese simply as *nan xun*.

Premier Li Peng continued to engage in passive resistance for some more time, using official documents to propose actions contrary to Deng's ideas. However, like a snowball gathering snow as it speeds down the hillside, from that point on the Party began to decisively align with Deng's vision. In June 1993, the Chinese leadership began calling for economic development based on high growth rates. Jiang Zemin declared that it was not necessary to put a label on reform by terming it as either capitalist or socialist. He coined the phrase 'socialist market economy' to define the direction of Deng's reforms. The Fourteenth Party Congress put its final stamp of approval on this idea between 12 and 18 October 1992. The next year in March, the National People's Congress (China's rubber-stamp legislature) enshrined Deng's mantra – that the central national task was economic development – into the Chinese Constitution. This was the definitive end to the debate over the direction of China's economy. It had taken three long years after 4 June 1989 for Deng to finally overcome the resistance to his policies. In the course of these three years, he had come perilously close to failure more than once. Deng could now withdraw into the political sunset.

Deng's southern tour remains the defining point from which China's economy, and consequently its influence, has grown to truly global proportions in the twenty-first century. From 1993 the Chinese economy grew in double digits each year until 2010. Foreign direct investment, which was in the single digits until 1991, averaged US $35 billion annually between 1992 and 1997 and rose even higher thereafter. Infrastructure development transformed the Chinese urban landscape. In March 1990, Deng had presciently observed changes in the global pattern after the Cold War also contained contradictions that China could use to its benefit and opportunities that could be taken advantage of. In order to do that, Deng called upon the CCP to think strategically and set long-term goals of doubling the national GDP by the end of the decade. He also underscored to his successors that the key to the success of economic reforms lay in maintaining political stability in China. Although Deng was convinced that the United States would work to subvert the CCP after its triumph against the CPSU, he recognized that China still needed the West in order to develop its economy. He, therefore, worked hard at keeping the lines of communication open with the West. Simultaneously, he deftly handled the immediate aftermath of the collapse of the Soviet Union. He avoided knee-jerk reactions. His advice to study the reasons for its collapse and to draw proper lessons was heeded by his successors. At the same time, he guided the Party and the state so that post-Soviet Russia was not left friendless and at the mercy of the West, by quietly restoring relations and urging his successors to utilize the situation to settle long-pending boundary and other contentious issues. In a precarious international and domestic environment immediately after the Cold War, Deng's wise handling of international affairs and the domestic situation after the Tiananmen Incident ensured that his successors could aspire to the dream of returning China to the world centre stage in the twenty-first century.

The notion that Deng Xiaoping had it easy after he became China's leader in 1980, because his power was absolute and unquestioned, which is advanced by way of explanation as to why China was able to modernize as quickly and efficiently, is far from the truth. The Party was riven with factions and deeply divided by policy differences, personal jealousies and power struggles. Despite Deng's position and power, he still had to navigate strong currents of internal opposition until the very end. His greatness lay in his ability to stay the course on reform and opening up, which he had outlined despite the many bitter battles he fought on economic policy with conservative forces. And he did so while maintaining the delicate balance between economic liberalization and political tightening so that the Chinese communists would not suffer the same fate as their Soviet cousins. He insisted that the absolute leadership of the Chinese Communist Party must be maintained at all costs. This, he always held, was the correct political line. In what is his final published speech, Deng warned his successors that 'if any problem arises, it will arise from inside the Party'.[35] Deng's words have never been forgotten by China's subsequent leaders.

:CHAPTER 2:

Quest for Prosperity

AFTER SURVIVING THE COLLAPSE OF COMMUNIST REGIMES IN OTHER parts of the world, and returning to the track of economic reform following Deng's southern tour in 1992, China embarked on two decades of spectacular growth. In 1992, China's GDP was about US $430 billion, less than a tenth the size of the American economy. By 2012, it stood at a staggering US $8.5 trillion, or more than half the size of the American economy. In 2011, it had already overtaken Japan as the world's second-largest economy. It had also overtaken Germany to become the largest merchandise exporter (exports were US $1.57 trillion), and it was the largest holder of foreign exchange reserves globally (around US $3 trillion). Between 1979 and 2010, China averaged an annual real GDP growth of nearly 10 per cent.[1] In effect, China literally doubled the size of its economy every eight years from 1979 onwards. This was not simply the by-product of an authoritarian system, though that helped in making it easier to implement the new economic direction without the sort of public debate or scrutiny that is common in democracies. What is important to note, however, is that such fundamental changes in economic policy were driven by the Chinese Communist Party itself. The Tiananmen Incident in 1989 had driven home the point that the Communist Party could no longer depend on the achievements of the so-called liberation period of its history (1921–49) in order to derive its legitimacy to rule China in the post-Cold War world. The protests of 1987 and 1989 had shown that the Chinese people had new socio-economic expectations. The Party began the difficult task of making the requisite adjustments to align itself to public expectations. The process was onerous, and even fraught with danger, because it involved changes not only to economic policies but to the Party's ideological moorings. The Party was very aware that erstwhile communist regimes in Eastern Europe that had tried to make such changes had been unable to stop the tide of political change from rolling in and washing away communism. The scope for error was small and the risk of failure was great.

Deng's final political intervention in 1992 had set the basic line – the Party would steer China away from the socialist economic model to a more market-driven model. This meant that the Party would need to turn its back on core socialist beliefs such as state ownership of all the means of production and the notion of the 'iron rice bowl'.*

This, in effect, meant the dismantling of the twin pillars of public ownership and the welfare system the Party had built

---

* The term 'iron rice bowl' was used by the Chinese philosopher and writer, Ji Yun (1724–1805). The Communist Party of China used the phrase to denote iron-clad commitments of providing life-long employment and universal welfare benefits to all Chinese. It was a key party slogan in the Maoist years.

after 1949, and of finding suitable alternatives for providing employment, housing and other social welfare benefits to the general population, without adversely impacting overall social and political stability. In 1993, the Party was, therefore, entering uncharted waters with untested human resources. Just twenty years later, it would not only survive the precarious transition despite two global economic crises (the Asian crisis of 1997–98 and the financial crisis of 2008–11) but succeed in doing so in a manner that also consolidated its grip on power.[2] How China's leadership skilfully navigated the risks of economic reform is, therefore, worth recounting.

The Party's immediate need was for a sound economic manager with sufficient political courage to steer the new economic direction set by Deng, and who could also deal with the deeply entrenched interests that were still resistant to change. The economic managers who had steered China through the first wave of reforms in the early 1980s – people like former General Secretary Zhao Ziyang and Xi Zhongxun (Xi Jinping's father) – were gone. The leader who quickly emerged as the most influential voice in economic policymaking in the post-Deng period was Zhu Rongji. Zhu was the outspoken leader of Shanghai City who, as both mayor and party secretary, had pursued a bold course to bring dynamism into the economy of China's largest city. Shanghai had been excluded from the first wave of reform and opening up (Deng later expressed his regret at the oversight). By the mid-1980s, the city government's fiscal revenues were low and there was an urgent need to draw down the excessive debts. After he took office as the mayor in 1987, Zhu articulated his vision for Shanghai's future, in terms of export-led manufacturing financed by foreign capital, and in partnership with foreign companies (this was at a talk at Fudan University in June 1988). He also spoke about the importance of labour mobility within China during a time when the Party still exercised very tight controls over rural-to-urban migration (known as the *hu kou* or household-registration system).³ These ideas were not simply bold but they also challenged boilerplate socialist economic principles at the time. But the Party's leadership recognized that Zhu's stewardship of economic policy was the need of the hour. He was quietly transferred to Beijing and given the overall responsibility for economic management, first as vice premier (1993–98) and later as the premier of the State Council (1998–2003). He brought his no-nonsense approach to bear on the problems that the economy faced. Zhu had no time for those who pandered to superiors or tried to second-guess them on policy, and could not be bothered with how well connected people were. He wanted to see results. He was reported to have once famously said at a conference of bankers that he heard some people had been using his name, claiming that they were good friends of his. 'Well, let me tell you, I don't know you,' he had thundered.⁴

If two words could describe what brought on the tectonic shift in the Chinese economic landscape after 1993, these would be 'competition' and 'decentralization'. The Party had already experimented with both of these ideas inside the four special economic zones (Shenzhen, Zhuhai, Shantou and Xiamen) since 1981, and decided now was the time to extend this to the twelve coastal provinces and two coastal municipalities (Shanghai and Tianjin) of China.*

'Competition' was introduced not simply as a backdoor entry to the reform of the state-dominated economic system but also in order to improve the efficiency of bureaucracy. This was a novel concept for a nation and population that had, for the most

---

* Sixty per cent of China's population resides in this region.

part, lived, worked and retired as per the dictates of the Party. 'Decentralization' was intended to ensure that local governments drove reform according to local conditions, and to reduce the scope for central authorities to massively intervene by forcing political objectives on provinces and localities that distorted the local economy, such as the Great Leap Forward (1958–62) had done, leading to many millions of deaths and a serious setback to China's industrialization process in the 1960s. To implement these two concepts was easier said than done because there would be strong resistance both within the Party and among the people, albeit for different reasons. For the ordinary citizen, this meant giving up guaranteed lifelong benefits, and for the party elite it meant the surrender of power and control. Inducting foreign capital and companies into China also left Zhu Rongji and his close advisors vulnerable to allegations of surrendering the country's economic sovereignty. The year 1993 was less than two decades down the road from the Cultural Revolution, when accusations of 'selling out' had meant deprivation of personal freedoms and even death. Careful political and ideological preparation could mean the difference between the success and failure of the new reform policy.

Zhu Rongji's first policy actions were designed to encourage the large-scale induction of foreign capital into China. Even he recognized that a direct assault on the state-owned enterprises (SOE, that is, the public sector) may be self-defeating until alternative means of production were in place. The reforms of the 1980s had already begun to attract a trickle of foreign direct investment (FDI) but what was needed was a significant uptick in the inflows. To secure this infusion of foreign capital, the leadership initiated key policies intended to give preference to foreign invested enterprises (FIE). These included more flexible labour laws that increased management's control over workers, including the hire-

and-fire of employees and wage benefits. Taxation and investment policies were also worked out to favour FIEs in order to reduce their business risks and to give them a clear path to profits. Foreign investors benefitted from the cheap and seemingly unlimited labour pool, the preferential treatment, and a predictable political system and policy environment that was not subject to change as a result of electoral cycles. The new policy also made provincial and local governments more aware of the benefits they could gain from encouraging foreign enterprises to invest in their localities – more jobs, more revenues and a higher profile. Those provincial and local authorities who worked to build an environment that was hospitable for business saw their revenues climb, while other localities lost economic activity and taxes. The workers also realized that in exchange for the surrendering of job permanency they were able to secure much higher wages by working for FIEs. The success of this policy may be gauged by the nearly tenfold increase of FDI inflows, which went up from US $6.6 billion in 1990 to over US $52 billion by 2000.

It is useful to examine how China did things differently from India in the 1990s when both were competing for foreign investment. Western investors who were beating a path to India would complain that they found it difficult to get meetings with the relevant ministers and senior officials. The Chinese would offer meetings with Premier Zhu Rongji and his top economic team. The Indian leadership disliked being lectured to by foreign CEOs about the challenges that their companies faced in the Indian economy, and possible policy options to address them. Chinese leaders, on the other hand, regularly invited groups of foreign CEOs to China and solicited their views (and criticism) in order to make them feel as if they were involved in the shaping of Chinese policies. In India, provincial leaders would expect the foreign investor to literally knock at their doors and ask for assistance as a favour. The Chinese provincial leadership were present at the airport with the red carpet to receive foreign investors and would accompany the investor throughout their trip as a sign of their eagerness to secure the investment. The Indian bureaucracy spoke only the language of administration (rules and regulations), and the Chinese officials spoke the language of business (facilitation). If the Europeans were critical of India on social issues or expressed concerns over the quality of life, we bridled at the insult. The Chinese quietly took the rap on the knuckles and secured European money, with no intention of paying more than lip-service to European values. In short, the Chinese worked their way into Western pocketbooks and wallets by showing their keenness to secure the investment, whereas Indians took the West for granted on the back of the potentially large Indian market. India needed to learn many lessons from China on attracting foreign investors.

Once the new policy had settled down and the provincial and local authorities had begun to see the benefits of encouraging foreign companies to establish joint ventures in their counties, the central government devolved greater decision-making powers to them and relaxed fiscal controls, thereby allowing them to find innovative means to attract more FIEs. The central authorities also reworked the fiscal relationship between the centre and the provinces by granting the latter higher rates of revenue retention. One study described this model as 'market-preserving federalism' – the creation of a hierarchy of governments with a clearly delineated scope of authority, greater decision-making authority with local governments over the supervision of economic activities in their jurisdictions, and the sharing of revenues between the federal and provincial governments.[5] This politically risky but managerially sensible 'decentralization' was what compelled even the laggards to compete. The old practice of securing fiscal resources from the central authorities, by using informal power networks based on the political lineage of provincial leaders or their connections in Beijing, came to an end. In December 1993, the State Council formally set rules for tax-revenue sharing between the federal and local governments (known as the Decision on Implementation of Management System of Taxes). Henceforth, the provincial leadership's financial resources would be pegged to its economic activities and would be proportionate to the revenues that it generated. This induced them to attract more foreign investment and increase productivity. In 1979, the first year of reform and opening up, the federal government controlled 51 per cent of all revenues. In 1997, this percentage was down to just 27 per cent, and the progressive provinces and localities started to reap significant financial reward.[6] The overall effect of these reforms was to align local governments more closely with local businesses and create new partnerships at the rural and township levels that could also absorb the excess rural workforce in a mutually profitable way. As a consequence of the twin policies of decentralization and competition, China's annual average GDP growth between 1992 (the year of the southern tour) and 1997 averaged 11 per cent.

In the early phases of the post-1989 reforms, the SOEs were largely untouched and even shielded from market forces (through quota and price controls). This dual-track approach minimized the likelihood of politically motivated attacks on Premier Zhu, as well as the possibility of widespread social instability in urban areas during the initial phase of market experimentation.[7] However, the drag on the economy as a result of poor economic performance by the SOEs meant that Premier Zhu could not postpone this reform for much longer. Tackling public sector reform was a huge challenge. It was not simply a question of tweaking shareholding or relaxing federal controls. It touched upon the Chinese Communist Party's core ideology of public ownership.[8] The SOEs were somewhat akin to the public sector in India that Prime Minister Nehru had called the 'commanding heights of the economy'. In China, this sector enjoyed the political support and patronage of the economic planners' group. Former Premier Li Peng (who still wielded power as the chairman of the National People's Congress) led the group that believed that the SOEs were the means to the Party's control over the economy, and that reforms might dilute such control and lead to the end of the its supremacy over time.

Despite the potential political opposition and the possibility of urban worker unrest due to lay-offs, General Secretary Jiang Zemin and Premier Zhu Rongji decided to take this particular bull by the horns after the new politburo was elected at the Fifteenth Party Congress in September 1997. (It was also decided at the this meeting that Zhu would replace Li Peng as the premier of the State Council in March 1998, thereby allowing him to assume full control over the administrative apparatus of the state.) They called their new policy 'grasping the large and releasing the small' or *zhangda fangxiao*. This policy released small- and medium-sized, state-owned companies from state control by allowing their ownership to pass into alternate hands, and was, therefore, another way of privatization. The CCP, however, could not call it that since the official party line was that it was pursuing a 'socialist market economy' (the phrase was coined by Jiang Zemin). It, therefore, had to opt for a disguised form of privatization (corporatizing small and medium SOEs) through a balancing act.[9] While releasing the small and medium enterprises, the Party repeatedly underscored how the public sector would remain the backbone of the Chinese economy since ownership of the large SOEs was still in state hands. Party members continued to be appointed to the top positions in the larger SOEs. This was intended to blunt allegations from the political opponents of SOE reform that the Party no longer controlled the economy, and also to allay concerns among the urban working class over potential job loss. Hence, the initial reforms in the large SOEs focused on the greater devolution of commercial decision-making powers and state support to help them compete in global markets. It was a mixed success. Really speaking, it was the 'release' of the small and medium-sized SOEs that had the effect of unleashing an economic tsunami in the coastal provinces of China, driven by the revival of the spirit of entrepreneurship and competition. Since the smaller SOEs were no longer under state control, they were able to tie up with foreign investors, and they also benefitted from the 'helping hands' of local government officials. This created a true private sector in China. The beginnings of the private sector in the mid-1990s marked a fundamental shift inside the party from a dogmatic emphasis on Maoist economics to a pragmatic market-driven approach. 'Although the rhetoric of socialism has been retained, the staunch anti-market, anti-private initiative, anti-private gain focus has been removed,' was how one Chinese scholar described the impact of Zhu's reform of the SOEs.[10]

The SOE reforms opened the floodgates to other changes. The period from 1998 to 2003 might rank as among the most productive in terms of economic policy in the Chinese Communist Party history. In December 1993, the State Council declared its intention to reform the banking system through the establishment of a central bank with the ability to carry out independent monetary policy. In 1998, a workable organizational structure for the People's Bank of China, along the lines of the US Federal Reserve Board, and a mandate to conduct monetary policy was finally crafted. In 1999, commercial banks were given greater decision-making powers and the legacy bad loans (NPA, or non-performing assets) of the four major banks (ICBC, China Construction Bank, China Agricultural Bank and Bank of Communications) were transferred to asset management companies.*

Foreign exchange reform also commenced in this period with the decision of the State Council in 1996 to begin the current account convertibility of the renminbi. One of the major reforms that Zhu initiated was the gradual abolition of all agricultural taxes (finally completed in 2005 by his successor, Premier Wen Jiabao), which pushed up rural incomes and consumption as well as productivity. Progressively bolder steps were also taken to increase the stakes for FIEs in the Chinese economy by allowing foreign enterprises to shift from purely export-oriented production to manufacturing for the Chinese domestic market as well. Finally, state-owned land was monetized and developed for infrastructure and urban renewal projects, leading to unprecedented levels of construction activity throughout China. As a result of the slew of reforms, China's nominal GDP grew from ¥2.69 trillion in 1992 to over ¥9.9 trillion by 2000, and per capita urban and rural incomes grew from ¥2,026 to ¥6,280 and from ¥784 to ¥2,253 during the same period.[11]

One of Premier Zhu Rongji's most difficult and politically risky tasks was to tackle the costly welfare system. Until the 1990s, the government carried out a 'full employment' policy in the urban areas and employees of SOEs or government units received comprehensive social benefits through their work units (*dan wei*). The Party's welfare model was based on the premise that all citizens

---

* Bank reforms were completed in 2004 with the conversion of the state-owned banks into share-holding entities, with the state as the largest shareholder.

contributed to society and the state in turn took care of their basic needs. Since the social benefits system was financed by the work unit and not directly by the state, the work units (SOEs) bore the heavy financial burden of providing comprehensive welfare for their employees. This system of welfare guarantees was known inside China as the 'iron rice bowl'. No Chinese leader before Zhu had tried to break the iron rice bowl, although Deng's reforms had begun the process. The big fear was that the ensuing social stability that had sustained the Party in power for half a century might shatter along with the breaking of the iron rice bowl. By the late 1990s, however, the Party did not have a choice. The taxation and budget reforms in the mid-1990s had reduced state subsidies to SOEs but they were still leaching money because of inflated payrolls. Public sector losses were becoming a burden on the state exchequer. According to one statistic of the roughly 76 million workers on SOE payrolls in 1993, a fifth of them, about 15 million, were redundant. In addition, the pensions of 20 million retired workers were supported by SOEs.[12] Housing and healthcare were also met from the SOE budget. (This was known as the *dan wei* system.) The choice before Zhu was to revive subsidy support to SOEs or to let go of some of the workers. He decided to bite the bullet in 1998. According to official Chinese data, over 25.5 million workers were laid-off between 1998 and 2001. To deal with laid off workers and to head off social unrest in the cites, they were initially sent to re-employment service centres which assured them basic livelihood expenses (consisting of a living subsidy, an unemployment insurance guarantee and a minimum living standard assurance, in case they remained unemployed beyond five years). The State Council also issued notifications for the improvement of social security systems, including a universal pension scheme and a new medical insurance scheme which became operational by the end of the 1990s. A massive public housing scheme was begun and subsidized purchase opportunities were offered to urban workers, thus removing an important factor for discontent. By one account, from 1998 to 2003, 477 million square metres of public housing space was completed.[13] Premier Zhu Rongji's consummate handling of complex reforms during his term from 1998 to 2003 was responsible for laying the foundations for China's economic growth in the next ten years, but during the two decades after 1989, the Chinese urban working class paid a heavy price for progress and bore the brunt of the burden of reforms, albeit with varying degrees of state support.

One major category of workers that could not access the new social safety net was the migrant worker. The disbanding of people's communes and the agricultural reforms of the early 1980s (household contract responsibility system)* had released millions of Chinese peasants for other tasks. Deng's industrial modernization programme in the mid-eighties brought these millions to the cities in search of work after 1985. Known as rural migrant labour (*nongmingong*), their numbers grew rapidly from about 30 million in the early 1990s to nearly 140 million by 2008. They formed the backbone of the newly established export industry and the manufacturing sector, in general.[14] Despite

---

* This system, introduced by Deng Xiaoping based on the experiments that Zhao Ziyang had conducted in Sichuan province in the mid-1970s, permitted the agricultural worker to secure a long lease on the land worked by him, and allowed him to sell some part of the production directly in the market. It had the dual effect of raising rural incomes through enhanced productivity and the sudden emergence of a large pool of surplus agricultural workers who had been let go by the people's communes and were, therefore, available to join the industrial workforce just as China was opening up.

the critical role of the migrant workers in the Chinese economy and though many of them had lived in the cities for a decade or more, they were not eligible for any urban welfare schemes. Their children could not secure educational opportunities in the cities, and they were not entitled to public housing only because they had not been officially registered as urban residents. Since the 1950s, the Party had developed an effective method of controlling the people by categorizing them according to where they resided and by restricting all socio-economic benefits only to the place of residence. It was called the 'household registration system' (*hu kou*). Those migrant workers who carried a rural *hu kou* were thus reduced to a second-class status in Chinese cities. Although this arrangement had blighted a whole generation of rural-turned-urban workers after 1985, it also created a large, easily exploitable, highly mobile and flexible industrial workforce for the Chinese economy without the attendant overhead costs of social welfare and housing. This is what had allowed China to keep wages so low over such a prolonged period of time that it attracted investors to pump billions of dollars into China's economy. China's urban wealth grew significantly during these thirty years, but it prospered at the expense of the *nongmingong*. They were visible in all Chinese cities, easily recognizable by their clothes, deportment and accent. They had left their families behind in the villages. They were permitted only an annual ten-day break to visit their families during the Chinese New Year. This is one of the major causes of the internal mass migration by millions of Chinese people that is still seen in China today around the Chinese New Year. After 1999 *nongmingong* were given access to pension insurance, and by 2003 they were accorded the status of working class, but the impact was limited because the household registration system prohibited their access to welfare and housing in cities. A party that prided itself as the party of the working classes mostly left the migrant workers of China to fend for themselves.

The rural workers were also bereft of social welfare benefits after the breakdown of the commune system in the 1980s ended their free access to education and healthcare. Since so few SOEs were located in rural areas, the new welfare schemes for urban workers had little impact in the countryside. The situation became so desperate that Premier Zhu warned his ministers at his final State Council meeting in January 2003 that 'urbanization has been interpreted as simply constructing more housing at low cost, seizing farmers' land and allowing foreign investors or domestic developers to move in without appropriately dealing with the farmers – this is a dangerous development.'[15] Belatedly, after 2004, the new leadership team of President Hu Jintao and Premier Wen Jiabao felt compelled to take palliative measures. In 2004 the State Council finally issued a white paper on China's social security and its policy, and in 2006 the Central Committee passed a resolution on building a socialist harmonious society that acknowledged the right of all citizens to education, employment, medical care, pensions and housing. Yet, the household registration system has not undergone any meaningful reforms till date and remains inherently discriminatory against the non-urban population in China. It is interesting to speculate on why the Party did not fear mass unrest among either the rural population or the migrant workers who had left the countryside to work in appalling conditions in the cities in the 1990s and early 2000s. One of the reasons might be that the Party did not see this group as being able to politically organize themselves (unlike urban workers) in any significant way as to pose a serious threat to the country's political stability. In the Party's experience, the 1987 and 1989 protests had been urban-centric with few ripples in the countryside. It, therefore, prioritized the building of a social welfare net for the urban working class.

Meanwhile, the Party also began the process of co-opting the newly emerged urban middle and entrepreneurial classes that identified with the Party's vision of economic development. In September 1997, General Secretary Jiang Zemin declared that any form of ownership that meets the criteria of supporting the development of productive forces can and should be permitted to serve the socialist market economy of China. In 1999, he went a step further when he declared that private entrepreneurs could now become members of the Communist Party of China. It was no longer to be a peasant, worker or soldier party; other social strata, the erstwhile so-called class enemies, could now join the Party.[16] Their inclusion into the national political mainstream was one more example of the remarkable ability that the Party displayed in the post-Tiananmen years to adjust their politics to the emerging reality. General Secretary Jiang Zemin and Premier Zhu Rongji showed flexibility and confidence in overturning core socio-economic principles of socialism while adeptly managing the political consequences, so that it would not lead to a repeat of the 1989 Tiananmen protests. This the Party was able to do through skilful political management in three ways. First, the ideological issues were finessed by describing the new economic policy as 'marketization' rather than as 'privatization' (*siyinghua*). Marketization, the Party claimed, was necessary in order to prepare the Chinese socialist market economy for global competition. The marketization policy was also introduced gradually and initially focused on creating a parallel market-oriented economy. The provincial and local governments were encouraged to experiment with foreign invested joint ventures and with rural and township enterprises, until they grew comfortable with the idea and saw that there would be no political blowback. This was quintessential Deng-ism – 'crossing the river by feeling the stones with the feet'. Second, as the new reforms began to gain momentum and some provinces and localities began to reap the benefits of their experiments, it started to generate envy in other provinces, and this automatically induced competition without the federal government's involvement. A similar approach was adopted with the SOEs as well. Instead of directly introducing a hire-and-fire policy for workers in SOEs, the Party first brought in flexible labour and wage laws for FIEs. Once these foreign or joint venture companies began to disadvantage the state-owned enterprises because of labour costs, it led SOE managements to demand a level playing field, thus leading to the adoption of laws written initially for FIEs being adopted for the whole national economy.[17] Eventually, this competition went right down to the grassroots, to the workers who migrated to provinces that offered the best chances for jobs, which in turn allowed the leadership in those provinces to arbitrage the availability of cheap, good-quality labour in exchange for attracting escalating volumes of FDI. Third, the Party cleverly aligned its economic reforms with the national interest. Nobody could accuse the leaders of selling out the country when the Party had declared that changes to the public ownership of means of production or the ending of permanency in employment were in the national interest. Anyone speaking out against these reforms risked being labelled as 'anti-party' and deprived of all benefits (schooling, housing, subsidized food, employment) that they and their families derived. In hindsight, the whole reform process gave the appearance of being seamless and stress-free, but in reality the political risks were very significant and failure was not an option. The system of collegial decision-making and collective responsibility that Deng had brought back after the death of Mao distributed that risk to some extent, but Zhu Rongji was still, in effect, riding the reform tiger all the while not knowing whether he was going to fall off and become the prey.

The initial successes of Zhu's reform policies brought on new problems. Indeed, there was little time for him and Jiang Zemin to savour the success of their reforms. Energy shortages began to plague the country as the economy grew. China had never needed to import foreign oil until 1993. Its oil imports quadrupled from 0.6mbpd (million barrels per day) in 1997 to 2.8mbpd in 2004 and doubled again to 4.7mbpd by 2010. As it became a centre of global manufacturing, its engine threatened to sputter and stall due to energy shortages. Besides, ever greater quantities of raw materials were also needed to feed the industrial machine. This triggered yet another new policy known as 'going out' (*zouchuqu*). The state, through its policy banks and diplomatic tools, supported the SOEs in a global hunt for resources. It became a full-fledged policy at the Party's plenary meeting in October 2000, and was enshrined in successive five-year plans beginning with the tenth plan (2001–05). The focus was almost exclusively on the developing countries. The objective was raw material extraction. It led to questionable business practices and ethics by Chinese companies as well as risky investments. Later on, such practices gave rise to allegations about China's 'extractive' behaviour (not that the Europeans had done it any differently in the eighteenth and nineteenth centuries). China's 'miracle' growth may not have been possible without such extractive activities. By 2009, over 30 per cent of global coal and iron ore, nearly 40 per cent of cement, and nearly 20 per cent of copper and aluminium was being consumed in Chinese factories.[18] It is easier in hindsight to put things neatly within a box by claiming that China had had a grand strategic master plan to 'colonize' African resources, but China's capture of global resources, at least in the initial phase, owes less to design and more to the demands of the domestic economy. It is true that the policy direction (*zouquchu*) was set by the Party and government, but many state-owned companies and banks were already operating autonomously (the result of SOE and banking reforms) and were driven by profit motives. It is also fair to say that raw material imports greatly helped foreign invested enterprises in China too. As long as this policy served the interests of the FIEs, criticism of Chinese actions in Africa and elsewhere by the rest of the world, and especially the West, was relatively muted. It was only when the Chinese economy was able to compete with Western economies in the late 2000s that the Chinese malpractices came to be spot-lighted.

It would be incorrect to say that there was no geostrategic element to the 'going out' policy as time went on. The Party had always thought in terms of its survival and promotion of its interests, and geopolitics was never far from the policy-makers minds. They were highly conscious of the perceived vulnerabilities arising from the overdependence of the Chinese economy on imported raw materials on which others had control.[19] With time, these anxieties grew within the Party leadership, leading President Hu Jintao to ultimately frame the problem as the 'Malacca Dilemma' in 2003, of which more is written in a subsequent chapter (see Chapter 5). From 2004 onwards, China's leaders took the strategic call that the direct ownership of raw material sources, as well as their means of transportation to Chinese ports would decrease both the economic (physical disruption in resource flows) and political (strategic blockade of sea lanes of communication) costs to China. In an effort to justify its predatory behaviour, the Party and state also started to raise the spectre of 'containment' of China by outside forces.

Of all the achievements that put China on the road to economic prosperity, the one that must rank at the top was its successful entry into the World Trade Organization (WTO). China had first applied for membership in the GATT (General Agreement on Trade and Tariffs), the predecessor of the World Trade Organization (WTO), in 1986. The export-led growth of the Chinese economy after 1993 increased the urgency of China's joining the multilateral trade facilitation body. President Jiang Zemin made this a major objective of the Party's diplomatic and economic strategy. He realized that American support was the key to facilitating China's entry into the WTO. If this particular key turned in the lock, the others (Japan and the EU) might not be able to resist China's entry into the global trading system. He, therefore, barnstormed America in October 1997 and talked up the market economy in China, the future of the non-public sector, and his wish to see even greater openness by China to the outside world.[20] All this was music to the ears of American businesspersons. One problem was the Clinton administration. On the presidential campaign trail, Clinton had painted China as a serial violator of human rights and freedoms, and linked doing business with China with this question. Jiang made it his mission to change Clinton's mind during their meeting in the White House on 27 October 1997. Jiang told Clinton everything that he wished to hear – that China was changing for the better, and how freedom was coming. China's development should be welcomed and supported since it would benefit the entire world. Change was only a question of time, he said. He cautioned Clinton that too much too soon might, however, risk internal chaos, which was neither in America's best interests nor China's. It is remarkable, in hindsight, how easily the Americans and Europeans bought China's line that if the West did not help it to economically develop while tolerating its political system, the whole world would stand to lose. This was a classic example of Chinese diplomacy – asking for something right away in return for promises it made to be fulfilled at some indeterminate time in the future. Clinton thought that he had a 'mutual understanding' with Jiang Zemin, and publicly pledged to do all he could to bring China into the WTO.[21]

Two other factors, serendipitously, helped the Chinese case. The first was the appointment of Zhu Rongji as the premier of the State Council in March 1998. The West considered him to be a 'reformer'. Others believe that initially Zhu was not enthusiastic about joining WTO, but later came to see that external pressure from the international community once China was committed to WTO rules and regulations would help him to weaken institutional resistance to SOE reforms.[22] The second factor was the Asian financial crisis of 1997-98. This crisis pushed China and America closer to each other. For China, domestic economic requirements led them to prioritize Western trade and investment and to engage more flexibly with the West. For America, the collapse of ASEAN economies led them to look at China as an alternative investment destination in East Asia. The process of bringing China into the WTO received a kick-start when President Clinton went to China in June 1998. This was the first American presidential visit since the Tiananmen Incident. The extent to which his personal views about China had changed between President Jiang's 1997 visit and his own visit several months later might be gauged from his memoirs. He wrote that he was 'strongly in favour of "bringing China into the WTO," in order to continue China's integration into the global economy and to increase both its acceptance of international rules of law and its willingness to cooperate with the United States and other nations on a whole range of other issues.'[23]

Initial negotiations did not go well. The Americans, according to Zhu Rongji, made unreasonable demands for the opening up of China's telecommunications and financial sectors as a condition to support China's WTO entry. He called the American behaviour 'very regrettable', but did not break off the talks.[24] In November 1998, Clinton revived the proposal for China's entry into the WTO in his letter to President Jiang Zemin and conveyed America's willingness to restart negotiations. The Chinese were pleased, believing that they might be close to reaching an agreement with Washington. In January 1999, Premier Zhu told the visiting chairman of the US Federal Reserve, Alan Greenspan, that he hoped to conclude the agreement on China's accession to the WTO during his visit to the United States in April 1999, and that he had already instructed his trade negotiators to open talks with the US Trade Representative, Charlene Barshefsky. He was assured by Greenspan that American business fully backed China's bid. 'Members of American economic circles, including myself,' he said, 'also hope that China will join the WTO as soon as possible.'[25] In February 1999, the Politburo of the Chinese Communist Party also approved the opening of negotiations as well as a raft of concessions that China might make. In April 1999, Premier Zhu Rongji came to America bearing the proverbial gifts.[26] He was to be disappointed. The inner machinery of the American political system had become deadlocked. According to President Clinton's memoirs, the deadlock happened because of the administration's desire for greater access to China's automobile market and China's unwillingness to commit to allowing the Americans to place limits on Chinese exports in the event of a Chinese export 'surge' that would undermine the domestic American industry. There might also have been political reasons for American hesitancy, namely the Clinton administration's concern that the United

States Congress, which was controlled by the Republican Party, might reject the deal as being inadequate, leading to great political embarrassment. US business was pushing Clinton to make the deal. They were appalled that the Clinton administration was more focused on extracting additional assurances from the Chinese in order to satisfy the US Congress instead of locking in the huge concessions that Zhu Rongji had offered. Clinton's advisors, on the other hand, including Robert Rubin, US secretary of the treasury, and Gene Sperling, director of National Economic Council, wanted more Chinese concessions. The almost-done deal fell apart. A disappointed Zhu left Washington, apparently encountering political headwinds when he landed in China. He was reportedly accused of selling out the Chinese (*mai guo zi*).[27] He offered to resign. Jiang refused to accept his resignation. The Chinese upped the ante by threatening to reverse the package on offer to the Americans.

The threat worked. At a high-level business interaction reportedly organized by the White House, American CEOs apparently rained criticism down on the administration for shrinking from a deal that would bring billions of dollars to America.[28] In the ensuing months, the American business leadership would exert continuous pressure until Clinton eventually buckled and threw principles to the wind. Eventually, he reneged and asked key negotiators, Charlene Barshefsky and Gene Sperling, to head to China in early November 1999, and to try and close the deal. Republicans and Democrats, including former US presidents Carter and Ford, were roped into the final push by the Clinton administration, and on 15 November 1999, the deal was finally done. In the short term, it brought immense economic benefit to America. In the long term, the American presumption that this deal would help anchor China–US relations and push the Chinese into being more amenable to accepting American hegemony was to be proved wrong.

It took a little longer to make the Europeans come around, but the Chinese used the same pressure tactics to whittle down the resistance inside the European Union. In March 2000, when Pascal Lamy, the EU commissioner for trade, came to Beijing, Zhu clearly told him not to expect any further concessions beyond what the Chinese had already given to the Americans. He reminded him that during the final negotiations with the Americans, he had not been deterred by their brinkmanship, including them checking out of their hotel rooms four times, apparently as a pressure tactic. 'Even if you were to change your air tickets five times and check out of your rooms five times,' Zhu told Lamy by way of warning, 'I would still make no concessions.'[29] Then, almost exactly as he had done with the Americans, Zhu held out the faint hope that China would change for the better in the future in ways that would make the West happy. 'Please give me time,' he said, 'and don't demand that I do this immediately. If you must demand that I do this, then we'll get stuck on this question.' Lamy tried to up the ante by hanging tough on the EU demands, for more Chinese concessions on auto tariffs and shareholding percentages in telecoms and insurance by emphasizing their political significance to European governments, only to be told by Zhu that he was elevating economic issues into political ones. In a classic ruse, he told Lamy that he had hoped to make friends with him (this was their first meeting) but that Lamy's attitude had made him wary. Lamy's persistence did eventually bring some concessions for the European insurance industry, but once the Americans had done the deal it became difficult for the EU to hold out for much longer. The China–EU deal on the WTO was inked in May 2000.

In hindsight, it is remarkable how successful the Chinese were in being able to convince the Americans and the Europeans to internalize the main Chinese argument, which was that for them to fully benefit from China's economy it was necessary to first grant permanent normal trading status to China. The West even used this Chinese argument as a justification for their legislatures when seeking approval for the deal. Clinton wrapped himself in bipartisan cloth, claiming that every American president since Nixon had worked to change China's behaviour and the WTO deal would 'work to pull China in the right direction.' He said that if America turned its back on this deal, it would almost certainly push China in the wrong direction.[30] Almost everything that Clinton professed would happen if America took the deal was subsequently proved to be wrong. Clinton talked about how the deal that he had concluded with China contained new safeguards against surges of Chinese imports, yet the trade deficit ballooned from US $83 billion in 2001 to US $367 billion in 2015. He had claimed that when the deal happened, America would be able to export products without exporting jobs – but this is not what happened. According to one estimate, 3.4 million American jobs were lost between 2001 and 2015 as a result of the trade deficit with China. US workers who were directly displaced by trade with China in this period lost a collective US $37 billion in wages as a result of accepting lower-paying jobs due to job loss, and the competition with low-wage workers in China who were manufacturing for the American market reduced the wages of 100 million US workers without a college degree.[31] In his speech at Johns Hopkins University, Clinton predicted the deal was good because, in time, ordinary Chinese would demand a greater say in their political affairs once they became prosperous, and that 'the Chinese government will no longer be everyone's employer, landlord, shopkeeper and nanny all rolled into one.' Instead, the political control inside China tightened in the ensuing years. And he derided China's effort to regulate the virtual world of the internet, mockingly wishing the Chinese good luck and adding, 'That's sort of like trying to nail Jell-O (jelly) to the wall.' It only goaded the Chinese to building bigger and better firewalls. Scarcely two decades later, his central argument – 'So if you believe in a future of greater openness and freedom for the people of China, you ought to be for this agreement. If you believe in a future of greater opportunity for the American people, you should be for this agreement. If you believe in a future of peace and security for Asia and the world, you should be for this agreement' – rang hollow.[32]

It has to be said that the Chinese entry into the WTO also brought huge commercial advantages to the West. The low cost of high-quality labour was leveraged by Western businesses to reduce costs and export products globally without losing competitiveness to rising Asian competition, especially from the ASEAN countries – Brunei, Cambodia, Indonesia, Laos, Malaysia, Myanmar, the Philippines, Singapore, Thailand and Vietnam – in the 1990s. American corporations made humongous profits. Chinese profits also helped the US economy. The Chinese trade surpluses that were reinvested into US Treasury securities (over US $1 trillion) enabled America to fund its budget deficits. Concerns over unfair trade practices, currency undervaluation, infringements of intellectual property rights and restrictive industrial policy were to surface only after the Global Financial Crisis when Chinese companies began to offer competition to the West in their markets. Therefore, if blame is to be apportioned on who let the Chinese tiger out of the cage, American and European leaders may need to own part of it.

The Jiang–Zhu era, as some put it, is a testimony to how 'bold reform is achievable when three conditions are present: a crisis of political credibility at home, vulnerability to an economic or financial crisis abroad and a leadership savvy enough to recognize the need for change.'[33] Faced with a political challenge that reflected the expectations of the Chinese people for significant change, the Party adjusted its ideology and policies to rebuild political credibility. The Party's economic experiments coupled with proper political management meant that despite the great burdens that it placed on the people, it was still able to win back popular support after 1989. Deng's advice to his colleagues to find new opportunities in every crisis was deftly used by his successors to push SOE reforms and other economic and administrative changes during the Asian financial crisis. If credit should go to one leader after Deng for making China what it is today, that would be Zhu Rongji. As a result of his pursuit of economic reforms despite the political risks, which his successor, Wen Jiabao, continued, by 2012 China's stock of cumulative foreign direct investment stood at a staggering US $1.3 trillion; its merchandise exports had grown from US $148.5 billion in 1995 to US $1.57 trillion by 2010 and, an outcome of the 'going out' policy, the cumulative stock of China's overseas investments in energy, minerals and infrastructure amounted to US $450 billion by 2012. It had secured control over significant portions of the world's raw materials, accumulated massive foreign exchange reserves and developed globally competitive companies by acquiring Western technology, management skills and even famous brands. All this was done without attracting hostile attention or making adversaries. The occasional notes of caution and the rare sounds of alarm were smoothened over by clever foreign policy. The world seemed to have sleepwalked into a possible Chinese century.

:CHAPTER 3:

Playing the West

CHINA'S SPECTACULAR ECONOMIC GROWTH AFTER 1993 WAS MATCHED by an impressive foreign policy that provided it the space and opportunity to rise in a swift manner within the existing global order. A rising power usually triggers anxiety throughout the international system. Beijing, however, largely avoided this for twenty years until after 2012. There were some concerns but, generally speaking, its rise was viewed with relative equanimity and even welcomed in large parts of the globe.[1] Deng laid down the basic guidelines for Chinese foreign policy conduct before he handed power over to his successors, yet equal credit should go to Jiang Zemin and Hu Jintao for the manner in which they evolved the foreign policy practice and crafted specific policies to help the rise of China in an uncertain international environment.

To fully comprehend the direction of Chinese foreign policy after 1990, it is important to go back to the summer of 1989. The Tiananmen Incident of 1989 had a much deeper impact on China's foreign policy than is popularly believed, because it affected relations with both the United States and Russia simultaneously. The Chinese communists had always been guarded about the US ever since the mid-1940s when the Americans had maintained a wartime liaison with them at their base in Yan'an during the Second World War. When they had tried to broker peace between the communists and nationalists, who were in power after the war had ended, Mao thought that the Americans wanted him to play second fiddle to Chiang Kai-shek , president of the Republic of China and leader of the nationalist party Kuomintang. He told an American journalist in September 1946 that American attempts at mediation were just a smokescreen 'so as to reduce China virtually to a US colony'.[2] By 1949 Mao's suspicions that the Americans wanted to sabotage the Chinese revolution had hardened into certainty. Though his relations with the Soviet communist party had also not been smooth sailing, Mao decided that the Americans were the bigger problem. He used the Soviet Union to deal with it. He announced that the soon-to-be-established communist regime would 'lean to one side' (the Soviet Union).[3] After the People's Republic of China was established, doubts and fears about America's intentions towards Communist China were further confirmed after US Secretary of State John Foster Dulles, in the 1950s, suggested the idea of using 'soft' policies to undermine the Communist Party in China. He claimed that the US and their allies were obligated to 'make every effort to facilitate the disappearance of that phenomena' (he was referring to communism) and 'to bring freedom in all of China by peaceful means'. This came to be known in communist parlance as the American strategy of 'peaceful evolution' (*heping yanbian*). Bo Yibo, one of Mao's closest comrades, recorded in his memoirs that Mao took Dulles's pronouncements very seriously and instructed all senior cadres to read them 'word-by-word with the help of an English dictionary.'

In January 1959, Mao Zedong prophesied that 'the United States is attempting to carry out its aggression and expansion with a much more deceptive tactic ...' In other words, it wants to keep its order and change our system. It wants to corrupt us through peaceful evolution.'[4] Mao's warning had resonated throughout the Party in the succeeding decades even when the Chinese moved closer to the United States during the years of the Sino-Soviet tension (1969–89). The Tiananmen Incident brought China's latent concerns about America back on to the front burner.

The Chinese leadership was convinced that the 1989 Tiananmen demonstrations were aided and abetted by the West. Deng said as much to Chinese American Nobel Laureate Tsung Dao Lee in September 1989. He noted that 'the West really wants unrest in China.'[5] Deng sent a clear political message to the Americans through former President Richard Nixon who visited China at his invitation in October 1989, saying that it was 'a pity that the US was so deeply involved in this matter ...'[6] – he meant the Tiananmen Incident. The fall of the Berlin Wall on 9 November 1989, and the collapse of communism in Europe probably reinforced their worst fears about America's future intentions towards communist China. Yet, Deng was aware that his strategic policy of reform and opening up might not be advanced without substantial American help. With the Soviet Union itself on the verge of disintegration, what China needed was a new foreign policy paradigm that enlisted American help to modernize the Chinese economy, while resisting American efforts to subvert the communist state. It was a daunting challenge made even more difficult because the end of the Cold War marked the global dominance of the United States. It also reduced China's earlier flexibility to manoeuvre between the two Cold War rivals by swinging like a pendulum in order to extract benefits from both the Soviets and the Americans in return for its support.

Deng Xiaoping's initial response to the rapid changes in the global order situation was to issue a three-line 'whip' to his party – observe the situation coolly, hold the ground and act calmly. 'Don't be impatient; it is no good to be impatient,' he said, 'we should be calm, calm and again calm, and quietly immerse ourselves in practical work to accomplish something – something for China.'[7] Through the autumn and winter of 1989, as regimes in Romania, Bulgaria, Czechoslovakia and East Germany disintegrated, the Chinese simply waited and watched. In March 1990, once the situation had stabilized to some degree in Eastern Europe, Deng told the leading members of the Central Committee to look out for opportunities amidst the crisis. 'There are disputes that we can use,' he said, 'conditions that are favourable to us, opportunities that we can take advantage of ... .'[8] He followed it up with two more critical pieces of advice at the Party's plenary meeting in December 1990. First, China should not seek to assume the Soviet mantle of upholding global communism; he reportedly said that 'we should not carry the great banner of socialism, nor are we able to.'[9] Deng was concerned that if the Chinese communists tried to pick up the baton that the Russians had dropped, they might become susceptible to attacks by the Americans, in a manner of speaking. Deng's second piece of advice was to avoid seeking global leadership. 'There is nothing to be gained by playing that role,' is what Deng told Party members.[10]

Deng is reported to have said, 'The city [China] is under siege; the enemy [America] is more powerful than us; regard defence as the main strategy.'[11] On the back of this advice, the Chinese Communist Party crafted a new America policy. In sum, the Party decided on a passive, non-aggressive foreign policy focused on furthering its strategic goal of economic development, and decided to keep a low international profile until China was strong enough to assume global leadership positions. This was captured in Deng's twenty-four-character strategy: 'observe calmly; secure our position; cope with affairs calmly; hide our capacities and bide our time; be good at maintaining a low profile and never claim leadership.' By the time his successors took over, the guiding principles of the new policy were non-alliance (*bu jiemeng*), non-confrontation (*bu duikang*) and no antagonism towards third parties (*bu zhendui disanfang*). Deng Xiaoping's successors, Jiang Zemin and Hu Jintao, would go on to build a successful post-Cold War foreign policy on these foundational principles, which would enable China to rapidly develop its economy with American help in spite of their deep-seated suspicions about America's intentions towards the Party.

While engaging the Americans, Jiang Zemin also worked on ways to strengthen the Party from subversion by the Americans. This was a delicate task because he had to do so while ensuring that the cadres understood that the Party needed to work with the Americans on the economy. After the Tiananmen Incident, the CCP launched a major campaign of 'patriotic education'. This involved rewriting the Party's history and reinventing its role. The central idea was to emphasize that China had been a victim of Western exploitation for almost a century until it was rescued from that state by the Communist Party of China. This 'victimization' narrative was embedded deep within the Party and state discourse as well as in the history books. The Party thus projected itself as the saviour of the Chinese people and the guarantor of China's dignity and self-respect. It coined a new slogan – 'rejuvenating the Chinese nation' (*zhengxing zhonghua*) – to suggest that with the Party in charge, the Chinese people could confidently look forward to reclaiming their place as the world's number one power. Since American help was still needed by the Chinese for economic development, which was critical for the Party's long-term plans, the narrative that senior leadership crafted after 1992 also allowed the Party to claim that so long as they were in charge, collaboration with the West would not be detrimental to China's independence and sovereignty. This way the Party under Jiang Zemin declared that it was both the purveyor of China's development and the protector of its sovereignty, thus reconciling its labelling of the West as an existential threat as well as a necessary opportunity.

After resolving the internal dilemmas on China's America policy, the next task for Jiang Zemin was to convince the US that it was in their own interest to help China to develop. The magnitude of the challenge that China faced at the time is little appreciated today. The new American ambassador, J. Stapleton Roy, who arrived in China in mid-August 1991, said in an interview many years later that the Tiananmen Incident had destroyed China's image in the United States. The Democratic Party had used China to attack President George H.W. Bush during his re-election run. In 1992 the new president, William Jefferson Clinton, came into office critical of China's human rights record and determined to link economic relations to an improvement in human rights.[12] Jiang's challenge was to persuade the Americans to put Tiananmen behind them because China was rapidly moving towards economic integration with the world in ways that would serve American objectives. To do that, the Chinese adopted an outwardly submissive and accommodative posture. A non-confrontational approach towards the Americans and the West, in general, thus became a key principle of Chinese foreign policy. The Chinese worked hard to reverse the negative perceptions caused by the Tiananmen Incident, by working with Ambassador Roy and with US business leaders to sell a more positive image to President Clinton. There were occasions when the carefully crafted Chinese policy threatened to unravel, such as when China fired missiles into the Taiwan Straits following the election of Lee Teng Hui, a pro-independence leader who was chosen as the first democratically elected president of Taiwan in March 1996. In that instance, China's show of force led to the deployment of American carriers in the Taiwan Straits and a stand-off with America.[13] It was to the Chinese leaders' credit that they were still able to keep Sino-American relations on their desired track.

Conscious that President Clinton, during his election campaign in 1992, had excoriated President George H. W. Bush for 'coddling dictators', Jiang decided to visit the United States in an effort to change American minds about China. It was an eight-day charm offensive from 26 October to 3 November 1997. He laid a wreath at Pearl Harbor to remind the Americans of their shared history in the Second World War. He visited colonial Williamsburg and donned a colonial hat to woo the American public, just as Deng had done at a Texas rodeo in 1979 by wearing a ten-gallon cowboy hat. He rang the opening bell for trading on the New York Stock Exchange to highlight China's support for capitalist practices. He even showed off his English language skills by quoting from famous American classics. By some accounts, he portrayed a buffoonish figure who liked to burst into song.[14] Yet, for all his outward appearances, Jiang Zemin clearly had a game plan in mind. Jiang's speech during the luncheon organized by the American China Society and five other organizations, on 30 October 1997, was tailored to perfection, hitting all the sweet spots of American hubris. He spoke about the newly emerging market economy and the role of the non-public sector, promised to open China even wider for American business, offered to hold 'democratic elections' and 'make policy decisions democratically,' to promote human rights, and to keep the Chinese military in a defensive posture.[15] President Clinton was thoroughly charmed. He wrote in his autobiography: 'I was impressed with Jiang's political skills, his desire to integrate China into the world community and the economic growth that had accelerated under his leadership ...,' and that 'he went to bed thinking that China would be forced by the imperatives of modern society to become more open, and that in the new century it was more likely that our nations would be partners than adversaries.'[16] He would not be the only American president to believe this to be the case. Other US presidents would also stay with the mistaken belief that China would eventually become more like America. The Chinese astutely played along. The most egregious example of China's skilful manipulation of the American public sentiment was when, on 4 September 2000, President Jiang Zemin recited parts of the famous Gettysburg address from memory in his interview with Mike Wallace for the TV programme *60 Minutes*.[17]

By the end of his visit Jiang had had done enough to secure a 'constructive strategic partnership' with the United States, and established a direct hotline (called presidential communications link) with Clinton (which incidentally was activated for the very first time after India tested its nuclear devices in May 1998), and had managed to convince the Americans that they could profit from helping China to develop its economy, though the American trade deficit already stood at around US $44 billion. Most significantly, Jiang extracted an assurance from Clinton that America would support China's application for membership of the World Trade Organization (WTO).[18] To allay concerns in some American quarters about the growing trade deficit, the Chinese declared that they would send 'buying missions'. Hundreds of Chinese businesspersons would descend on America and pledge to make purchases in billions of dollars just before high-level visits. During the summits themselves, there would be deal-signing ceremonies and impressive public pronouncements in the presence of Chinese and American leaders. Such pledges were seldom fulfilled by the Chinese after the visits had happened, but by the time the Americans had figured that out the Chinese had already secured their own objectives. This was a pattern that China would adopt in its dealings with all countries with whom it was running large trade surpluses. The Chinese understood the importance of optics in democratic societies, and they played on the hopes of their opposite numbers, of getting eventual access to their megamarket, in order to wrest concessions that benefitted the economy and the Communist Party of China. The Americans convinced themselves that it was only a matter of time before China became a responsible stakeholder in the US-led global order. Meanwhile, on Jiang Zemin's watch, the Americans invested billions of dollars into the Chinese economy, transferred key technologies for its modernization and helped secure China's entry into the WTO.

By the end of the 1990s, Jiang's foreign policy had been able to largely remove the stain of the Tiananmen Incident, secure capital and technology from the US for China's development and win international respectability. So long as they were pursuing all these goals, the Chinese kept their counsel, accepted American tutelage and pretended to adapt to the new US-led world order. As China's economy began to power up, the Chinese began to push back. This pushback fitted in well with the Party's new strategy of channelling nationalistic feelings into ways that would bolster its credentials as the political force that was best placed to protect China's sovereignty and dignity. The perceived American bullying during the US–China face off in the Taiwan Straits in 1996 had aroused nationalistic feelings inside China, and such feelings were encouraged by the publication of books like *China Can Say No* (*Zhongguo Keyi Shou Bu*), which accused the Americans of acting narcissistically and doing everything possible to halt China's rise. The book had reportedly sold two million copies.[19] The Party's experiment with nationalism as a diplomatic pressure tactic started on 7 May 1999, during the American bombing campaign on Serbia during the Kosovo crisis, when American long-range B-2 bombers from Whiteman Air Force Base in Missouri delivered GPS-guided bombs that hit the Chinese Embassy in Belgrade, killing three Xinhua News Agency reporters. The Americans claimed that it was a genuine targeting mistake due to faulty maps. The Chinese maintained that they had been deliberately targeted. The bombing was used by the Party to stage a state-supported backlash against America on the streets of Beijing. Thousands of Chinese students descended upon the American Embassy (then located at Xiushuijie Street, a stone's throw from the Indian Embassy), shouting 'blood for blood' and other hate-filled slogans. Posters of President Clinton depicted as a devil with horns were pasted on the walls all over the city. They pelted the embassy with bricks, shattering most of the glass on its façade. The exits were blockaded to American diplomats, who were forcibly bottled up inside the building for days. The People's Armed Police, who stood guard in front of the American Embassy, made little effort to control the mob. There was no doubt that this situation had the Party's support because the crowd had gathered after Vice President Hu Jintao went on national television, calling the bombing 'criminal' and 'barbaric' and likening it to an attack on China's sovereign territory. China neither waited for the outcome of the investigation into the bombing, nor did its leaders take phone calls from the American president until eight days after the incident. When President Clinton, after first unsuccessfully trying to contact President Jiang Zemin on the hotline, made an impromptu televised apology on the airport tarmac en route to inspect the floods in Oklahoma, a senior Chinese academic dismissed it as 'I'm sorry I stepped on your foot in the bus kind of an apology.[20] The Party followed a similar methodology in April 2001 when a US Navy EP-3 surveillance aircraft collided with a Chinese PLAAF F-8 fighter aircraft over the South China Sea. The collision was caused when the Chinese fighter aircraft dangerously challenged the US aircraft during a Freedom of Navigation and Overflight Operation (FONOP) in the South China Sea. The Chinese plane and pilot were lost at sea. The Chinese pilot had seemingly provoked the collision but, as far as the Chinese government was concerned, he was the tragic victim who had died while valiantly defending Chinese sovereignty from American provocation. The official Chinese version created a wave of nationalistic hubris among the Chinese public. When there was the inevitable public outcry, the Chinese government used it to extract benefits from the Americans. Thus, when the damaged US plane force-landed on a Chinese military airfield in Hainan Island, its crew remained in Chinese hands for eleven days until the American government apologized in writing to the Chinese people.

On both occasions, the Chinese seized on random incidents to incite nationalistic feelings in the people and backed the subsequent public outcry to bring pressure on the opposite party to concede and, equally importantly, to bolster the Chinese Communist Party's nationalist credentials. Once the demonstrations had served their purpose from the Party's perspective, the security forces moved in to shut them down. Such actions served the purpose of demonstrating to the Chinese people that the Party could stand up to bullying by foreigners and this helped it to build its post-1989 narrative as the defender of China's dignity and honour. Over the years, this tactic has been used against other countries as well to a similar effect. In almost every instance, China would claim it was the victim, and demand an apology and reparations. The Party would then claim that it had redeemed the honour of the Chinese people. Officially sponsored nationalism, thus, became a legitimizing force for the Chinese Communist Party.[21]

In the beginning, some China experts tended to suggest that such behaviour was a reaction or a response to provocation by others. It was assumed that the virulent nationalism in China was a consequence of the shame and humiliation that it felt as a result of its treatment at the hands of the West during the 'century of humiliation'. It was, therefore, thought that over time, this would be a declining factor in Chinese foreign policy as the country's economic and military power grew.[22] Such views tend to overlook or downplay the domestic political factors behind China's behaviour and ultra-nationalist actions. As a consequence, relatively fewer voices were heard in this period calling out the Chinese for their attempts to whip up ultra-nationalist feelings. Chinese experts quickly picked up on this sort of narrative.[23] It took some time for the mainstream to recognize that the form of nationalism that the Chinese Communist Party practised was not merely affirmative but aggressive. It identified very specific enemies against whom it wilfully aroused public anger and mobilized demonstrations. This was part and parcel of the Party's new avatar. It was using patriotism (*aiguo zhuyi*) as a tool to leave the Chinese population with a constant sense of being besieged and beleaguered from the outside and to project the Party as the only protector they could depend upon.

China's foreign policy for the rest of the Western world during Jiang Zemin's presidency more or less mirrored their policy towards the United States. Like the US, on 27 June 1989, the European Council had harshly condemned the so-called

Tiananmen massacre as 'brutal repression,' and had followed the American lead in freezing relations and imposing economic restrictions. Consequently, trade fell from a high of US $23.51 billion in 1990 to US $11.6 billion the following year. Soon enough, however, the Europeans learnt of the secret US–China negotiations to bring the relationship back on track under President George H.W. Bush, who sent his special envoy, National Security Advisor Brent Scowcroft, to China twice in 1989, and became anxious that they might miss out on commercial opportunities. China manipulated such anxieties to work themselves back into European favour. By the end of 1994, with the exception of the arms embargo, all other European restrictions imposed on China after the 1989 incident had been revoked. In 1995, the European Union released its first policy paper on China, titled 'A Long-Term Policy for China-Europe Relations', the centrepiece of which was the policy of 'constructive engagement'. For stressed European businesses that were facing a difficult post-Cold War readjustment, China rapidly became the focus of European commercial policies because of its large market and cheap labour. The problem for the European capitals became one of how to finesse the issue of human rights, so it did not look as if they were sacrificing human rights to the interests of European business. They claimed that although human rights in China remained a matter of serious concern, European objectives would be better served based on persistent communication with the Chinese than on punitive measures.[24] European governments claimed that China was making serious efforts to integrate into the global order and should not feel pressurized, and should be allowed to adjust at its own pace. Hence, their policy was of 'constructive engagement' with China, which to them meant that they were not abandoning human rights but simply engaging in a 'silent dialogue' on the matter.[25] After a while, even this so-called silent dialogue was quietly outsourced to the European Union, which had no real diplomatic power to effect changes in Chinese behaviour. National governments in Europe, meanwhile, fully aligned their China policy with national economic interests.*

If the European approach to human rights in China seemed hypocritical, especially when they were mounting pressure on India over alleged human rights violations in Jammu and Kashmir, nobody in Europe appeared to care.

In return for the Europeans showing 'understanding' and acceptance of China's political system, China threw open its markets to European products and investments. Between 1994 and 2002, trade almost trebled from US $31.52 billion to US $86.75 billion, while FDI touched US $20.9 billion in just four years (1998–2002). Germany led the way. The Germans were still coping with the economic costs of reunification** and their economy had become dependent on foreign trade. A succession of German chancellors – Helmut Kohl, Gerhard Schroeder and Angela Merkel – opened the door to doing business with China and threw away the key. Backed by the wealth and authority of the federal government, German companies, led by their leading automobile and construction equipment corporations, eagerly moved into China to take advantage of the potentially huge business

---

* The French were so eager to secure an Airbus deal that they even blocked a Danish effort to sanction China over human rights in the UN Security Council in 1997–98.
** On 3 October 1990, the two Germanies – the German Democratic Republic (East Germany) and the Federal Republic of Germany (West Germany) – which had been separated since the end of the Second World War in 1945, were reunited at the end of the Cold War. The cost of German reunification was in billions of dollars.

opportunities that they saw. In the early 1990s, the patriarch of Volkswagen, Ferdinand Piech, grandly declared that 'we are going to get the Chinese off bicycles'.[26] Volkswagen, Bayer, BASF and the *mittelstand* – German SMEs who were the hidden champions – made the long bet on China, raking in billions for the German economy. Premium scientific establishments like the Max Planck Institute and Fraunhofer opened their doors to China's research and development institutions, giving them access to state-of-the-art scientific and technical knowledge. German policy amounted to a technology-for-markets swap. Chancellor Schroeder (1998–2005) claimed that this approach was going to change China – a strategy that he labelled as 'change through trade' (*Wandel durch Handel*). His foreign minister, F.W. Steinmeier coined the phrase 'community of responsibility' (*verantwortungsgemeinshchaft*) to describe China–EU ties, suggesting that a closer relationship with EU might make China a more responsible member of the global community. Perhaps, the Germans believed that their successful experience of *Ostpolitik* (change through rapprochement) with the Soviet Union might be transferred to their dealings with China.[27] Such was the optimism about China becoming a like-minded member of the international community with shared values that German Chancellor Schroeder is believed to have contemplated the sale of a Siemens-built plutonium plant near Frankfurt to the Chinese, while the Germans were busy preaching the sins of nuclear proliferation to India. And the cherry on the cake for the Chinese was a strenuous effort by the Germans and the French from the end of the 1990s to plead to the Americans to lift the arms embargo within a few years after the Tiananmen Incident, (The Americans refused to agree.)

China's European policy was based on a three-pronged strategy. First, they took advantage of the mismatch between their own centrally controlled economy and the West's open economies to fully exploit opportunities in European markets, while protecting their market with industrial policies and restricted access. All this time, they kept promising unspecified market liberalization at some indeterminate time to keep the Europeans hoping. In the process, the EU gave significant access and benefits to China while securing too little, too late. Second, the Chinese cleverly channelled European pressure on matters like human rights into a Human Rights Dialogue with the European Union in 1996, as well as a Rule of Law Dialogue with the Germans in 1998. This allowed the Chinese to keep up the pretence of engaging with the West on human rights issues through institutionalized frameworks, but actually turned them into 'inconclusive talking shops'. Third, the Chinese learnt to exploit divisions within the Western world and made them compete amongst themselves for Chinese favours.[28] The Chinese would pledge to buy Airbus aircraft just before a visit by the French president or German cars just before a Chinese leader went to Germany in such big quantities that European and American businesses began to put pressure on their governments to accept unreasonable or excessive Chinese demands, simply to allow powerful companies to jump on the bandwagon. If any European state stepped out of line, like France did in 2008 when it received the Dalai Lama, swift retribution followed. The Chinese would punish the erring European states where it hurt them the most – business and summitry. In this particular case, the Chinese cancelled the China–EU annual summit, and punished all European states for the transgression of one, in order to build internal pressure on the offending European state to fall in line and to send a clear message to the rest : if they failed to rein in the errant European member, the entire EU would bear the consequences.

The Chinese also cleverly tried to drive a wedge between the Americans and their European partners by publicly supporting the European Project (European integration). China saw this as an easy way of playing to the European ego. The Chinese declared the Europeans to be a 'major force in the world', and from 1998 began annual summits with them. In September 2005, they declared that they had a strategic partnership with the EU. The Europeans were also delighted when the People's Bank of China agreed to diversify its foreign currency reserves by increasing the Euro component, little realizing that it served Chinese interests to build the Europeans into a separate and independent pole in the American-led world order. The fallout between the Americans and the Europeans over the invasion of Iraq in 2003 was also used by China to divide them.[29] It was only around 2009 that the Europeans realized that they were being manipulated. By then, the Chinese had gained access to some of Europe's most sophisticated technologies and created massive competition in the businesses that the Europeans were good at. One German official bemoaned that the Chinese 'are buying the backbone of German innovative capability'.[30] European trade deficit grew from €55 billion in 2002 to €169 billion by 2009. Issues of market access, artificially keeping the renminbi (Chinese yuan) low and intellectual property rights violations began to surface regularly in China–EU dialogues. Having helped to steer China into the WTO, they discovered that they now had less leverage to get China to address their concerns. As European economies became more dependent on China, it was used to punish the Europeans who crossed the red lines set by China with economic sanctions. Two decades after the Europeans had imposed sanctions on China, the Chinese started to use sanctions as a tool against their erstwhile 'tormentors'. By the time the West realized that they were being played, China had succeeded in gaining international diplomatic space, accessing foreign funds and securing Western technologies. The success of their strategy with the West is what made it possible for China to treble its economy between 2000 (US $1.8 trillion) and 2010 (US $6.09 trillion) and to overtake Japan as the world's second-largest economy. This must be regarded as a strategic foreign policy success for the Communist Party of China.

While engaging with the West, the Chinese were simultaneously troubled by the collapse of the Soviet Union and highly aware of American efforts to bring the new Russian Federation into the Western order. Every Chinese leader has talked about this problem, and lessons from the Soviet collapse in 1991 continue to shape domestic and foreign policies right up to the current times. The disintegration of the Soviet Union had eliminated an immediate threat for China, but in the post-Cold War period, China also needed Russia as a counterbalance to American hegemony. It could not countenance the total collapse of Russia. Therefore, in March 1990, Deng Xiaoping declared that China and the Soviet Union must remain as independent poles in the new global order,[31] and his successor Jiang Zemin began reaching out to Boris Yeltsin. The new Sino-Russian relations were, initially, more a marriage of convenience, because President Yeltsin was looking towards the West. Despite this, China quietly settled the border with Russia – the boundary agreement was finally ratified in 2005, and demilitarized it – both sides withdrew their forces one hundred miles away from the border and reduced heavy armaments in 1996) in order to neutralize any threat from the north and to minimize the possibility of the Americans co-opting Yeltsin into 'containing' China. A second critical objective vis-à-vis Russia was also secured in the late 1990s – the Chinese gained direct access to sophisticated Russian weapon platforms and technology after the

West had embargoed arms exports in the wake of the Tiananmen Incident. Finally, the Russian accommodation of Chinese interests in Central Asia, a region of perceived vulnerability for China from the perspective of its restive Islamic population in the northwestern territories (Xinjiang Uyghur Autonomous Region) and the possibility of American and NATO military entrenchment in Central Asian areas contiguous to China, afforded them a measure of comfort and security. For all these reasons, the Chinese persisted in their relations with the Russians despite Boris Yeltsin's firm focus on the West.[32]

The Chinese kept this steady acceleration of diplomatic activities with Moscow mostly under the radar. In 1996, for example, when the two sides declared a 'strategic cooperative partnership,' the Chinese were careful to avoid portraying it as a security alliance. Russia, for them, was part of the bigger and longer-term strategy of dealing with the United States. Hence, they kept the relationship with Russia out of the public eye. It was only after their key objectives vis-à-vis the United States had been secured – Congress voted to normalize trade relations with China in September 2000 and the US–China Relations Act 2000 was signed into law by President Clinton on 10 October 2000 – that the Chinese finally sealed their strategic partnership with Russia by concluding a twenty-year Treaty of Good Neighbourliness, Friendship and Cooperation in July 2001. In the first decade of the twenty-first century, the new leaders of China and Russia, presidents Hu Jintao and Vladimir Putin built upon the above-mentioned treaty and steadily expanded it into new commitments that covered the entire gamut of ties – joint military exercises, a sizeable enhancement in trade, an energy partnership and a deepening convergence on the shape of the international order in this century. A group of American experts has described the relationship as gravitating from tactical accommodation to one of strategic value by design from the Chinese perspective.³³

Jiang's thirteen-year leadership of the People's Republic of China finally came to an end in early 2003. At the time that he demitted the office of president, China had fully normalized its relations with the West, repaired ties with Russia, India, Vietnam and Japan, and had begun to expand its diplomatic influence into Africa and Latin America. Noted China scholar Evan Medeiros from the United States summed up Chinese foreign policy under Jiang Zemin as being conducted through three lenses. First, China portrayed its claim and efforts to be a great power as legitimate because it was based on history. Second, China made itself out to be a victim of others' greed and exploitation, and thus all its actions were presented as reasonable responses to infringements of its dignity, sovereignty and territorial integrity. Third, China successfully convinced much of the world that it would not pursue expansionism or hegemonism, and thus earned the world's trust. This allowed China, for two decades between 1995 and 2015, to avoid confrontation while denying the Americans the capacity to 'contain' them, and to cloak their aggression and assertiveness as a defensive response mechanism, until the gloves finally came off in 2015.³⁴

When Hu Jintao took over as the president of China in March 2003, it was time to step out onto the world stage in a more decisive way. The China that Hu Jintao inherited from Jiang was prosperous and influential in the world. The trauma of Tiananmen was behind them, and power inside China had been transferred in the manner the Party had wanted. Deng's strategic guideline of 'hide and bide' was still the official guideline of China's foreign policy, but a subtle shift had already started and Hu helped the process along.³⁵ The twin objectives of pursuing economic modernization and diminishing the American capacity to 'contain' China, which Deng and Jiang had pursued since 1989, remained unchanged. But Hu added a third objective – to adjust China and the rest of the world to China's new role as a major power. This was the transition phase in Chinese foreign policy – from passive looker-on under Jiang Zemin to active shaper of world events under Xi Jinping. Hu Jintao recognized that China still could not afford to frontally challenge the Americans until it had a powerful economy and a strong military. He understood that this might take a few more years to do. In the meantime, it was important that China continue strengthening itself by any means, but that risked red flags being raised against it by its neighbours. Hence, Hu's mission was to try to 'take the menace out of China's rapid growth' by convincing the international community that they stood to benefit from China's rise.[36]

Zheng Bijian, one of Hu Jintao's close advisors, coined a new slogan in 2003 to describe the new Chinese role in the world. He called it 'peaceful rise' (*heping jueqi*). This idea justified China's rise by assuring the rest of the world that it would be peaceful and that China was not striving for hegemony.[37] Zheng Bijian publicized his idea at the annual Bo'Ao Forum in October 2003. (China holds an annual economic conference in Hainan, modelled on the lines of the World Economic Forum at Davos.) The idea of 'peaceful rise' gained support when Premier Wen Jiabao referred to it in his speech at Harvard University in December 2003. By mid-2004, however, the phrase had vanished from public discourse. It was replaced with the phrase 'peaceful development'. Chinese experts claimed that this was merely a change in style, not substance, and that the issue was simply one of finding the appropriate terminology. However, in reality, it was much more than that. China had, uncharacteristically, revealed its true intentions. Its deception had been unmasked briefly. The aggressive nationalism that it had begun to display in the region since the end of the 1990s was starting to create unease. The 'China threat' narrative was gaining ground.[38] In such circumstances, the impression that the new phraseology sought to create of a rising China threatened to tip over the apple cart, before China's economic and military capabilities had reached the appropriate level of sophistication to withstand American pressure. China's leaders, therefore, quickly pulled back from the little experiment and returned to Deng's gold standard of 'hide and bide' for a little while longer. Two years later, at the Central Conference on Work Relating to Foreign Affairs in August 2006, the new idea of a 'harmonious world' was introduced into the Chinese foreign policy lexicon. The idea had overtones of peace and universal brotherhood; it muted the element of challenge and instead portrayed China as a responsible power that was ascending the ladder of the international system in harmony with others. It seemed to provide reassurances but did not specifically spell these out; it diverted attention from China's military modernization and especially its naval expansion; it lulled the West into thinking that China would accommodate itself within the existing world order; and, most significantly, it allowed the Chinese to play the role of a responsible, constructive and virtuous major power in contrast to the Ugly American.* In short, Chinese leaders were able to keep relations with the US on an even keel in order to create a stable international environment for China's economic take-off, without lowering their guard against the Americans whom they perceived as an existential threat right from

---

* Public perception about the US in the Indo-Pacific region after the American invasion of Iraq in 2003 and the prolonged presence in Afghanistan after the elimination of the Taliban was turning negative.

the start.[39] Jiang Zemin and his successor, Hu Jintao, essentially bought time while China shaped a new organizing principle for its foreign policy to replace Deng Xiaoping's foreign policy of 'keeping a low profile and biding time' (*tao guang yang hui*). Thus, it was only after the onset of the Global Financial Crisis, when China felt that the West had had a setback, that this key principle in handling China–West relations was abandoned, and China transitioned from a policy of passive adaptation to proactively shaping the regional and global environment to reflect its preferences and interests.[40] By then, China's economic strength, military power and diplomatic influence had been significantly enhanced. It would permit Xi Jinping, his successor, to evolve a fundamentally different direction in Chinese foreign policy under a new organizing principle: 'striving for achievement' (*fenfa youwei*).

:CHAPTER 4:

Wooing the Rest

WHILE THE WESTERN WORLD ENGAGED IN TRADE AND BUSINESS THAT was mutually profitable for both sides in the two decades after 1990, the developing world was also looking towards China for economic benefits – for trade, finance and expertise. China was initially interested in prioritizing its relations with the West, but by the end of the 1990s a combination of domestic and international circumstances put China on the road to rapid development of relations with the rest of the world. Hence, when Chinese policy and actions grew more robust and assertive and raised concerns in Washington and Western capitals by the mid-2000s, China's rapid rise was not viewed by the rest of the world in a similar manner, and its pushback against the West was even welcomed in other parts of the globe.[1] Why did China's rising power not trigger anxiety among its neighbours and in the Indo-Pacific region? How had this divergence of views on China emerged even in geographies and among countries that were aligned to the West, or were seen as being important to American and Western interests?

The United States was the dominant power in the Western Pacific at the end of the Cold War. The Association of South-East Asian Nations (ASEAN) regarded it as the guarantor of regional security and economic well-being. China's presence was quite small and still relatively new. China's support for local communist insurgencies in Indonesia, Malaysia, the Philippines and Thailand in the 1950s and 1960s, as well as its more recent assertiveness in the South China Sea had not been forgotten. Yet, scarcely two decades later, China would match the American influence in this region, leading a US Congressional Research Service (CRS) report in 2006 to remark that 'few major international relationships have changed so much or as quickly in recent years ... having been transformed from one of suspicion and fear, driven at first by ideology and then largely by ongoing territorial disputes, to one of increasing cooperation and collaboration'. What had happened to shift the balance so quickly? Was it due entirely to skilled Chinese diplomacy, or did US actions also play any part?

Throughout the Cold War, the Americans had had a strong and effective alliance network in Southeast Asia. After the Soviet Union was vanquished, these alliances appeared to become redundant. Many Americans questioned the need for high levels of military commitment in Southeast Asia and felt that ASEAN should bear greater financial responsibility for the continued American presence. America's priorities gradually shifted northwards to the Chinese market as it opened up after 1990. From America's perspective, China's opening-up not only reduced the geostrategic salience of Southeast Asia, but, more surprisingly, the Clinton administration also began to focus attention on the state of democracy and human rights in the region. ASEAN governments and elites felt vulnerable and they began to initiate new regional initiatives like the ASEAN Regional Forum (ARF) in order to reinforce their sense of regional security. During this time, changes were also happening in China's approach towards Southeast Asia. For both political and economic reasons, there was a strategic re-evaluation in Beijing. China declared that it had no political interests in Southeast Asia – in other words, they would not support communist parties or movements in ASEAN countries – and claimed to follow a 'good neighbour' approach. This process was aided by the sharp uptick in trade between China and ASEAN in the mid-1990s.

The real shift in the regional balance of power started with a black swan event in 1998, euphemistically known in East Asia as the 'Asian flu' (the Asian financial crisis). Currency devaluation and consequent capital flight from the region in 1997 and 1998 weakened and destabilized ASEAN economies. Within days, the Indonesian rupiah, the Thai baht and the Malaysian ringgit lost over half their value. The Southeast Asian governments turned to the West for assistance through the Western-controlled International Monetary Fund (IMF). The IMF's conditions for a bailout were severe and were considered not merely intrusive but even insensitive. Prime Minister Mahathir Mohammed of Malaysia became the symbol of regional defiance after he rejected the IMF's bailout conditions. Despite the severity of the economic crisis in several countries that regarded themselves as America's allies and partners, the US seemed unwilling to help them. China seized the opportunity. It did three things, all essentially in its own economic self-interest, but portrayed them to the Southeast Asian countries as important 'concessions' that China was making in order to help out ASEAN. First, China pledged not to devalue its currency (renminbi) so that ASEAN products remained competitive; second, it offered a financial bailout to Thailand and Indonesia with no strings attached; and third, it went on a diplomatic charm offensive to convince the entire region that China was a positive influence and a stabilizing regional force. By seizing on the American indifference to economic difficulties in Southeast Asia, China was quickly able to reverse the region's previously negative perceptions about it.

China consolidated its position still further once ASEAN economies began to recover, by offering them short-term bridging loans and long-term market support in the form of an ASEAN–China Free Trade Agreement in 2002. It concluded an agreement on trade in goods with ASEAN as a whole in November 2004, throwing open Chinese markets for ASEAN products under reduced tariffs and allowing for Chinese investments to flow into Southeast Asia. (This was also the time when Japan appeared to be pulling away.) It did not raise labour or human rights issues as conditions for economic help. China's actions during this period were described as based on 'communitarian requirements of order over individual preferences of freedom'.[2] As a result, by the time the twenty-first century dawned, ASEAN unease over China's politico-security domination of the region went subterranean, and China took the driver-seat among the regional economies. China's policy also had a strategic message. The message to the region was that China had ASEAN's back while the West had turned them away. Conscious that the existence of maritime disputes might mar China's carefully cultivated benign image, it also made a tactical offer to talk about the South China Sea in a multilateral forum (which China had resisted so far). In fact, such an offer amounted to opening a talk shop, similar to that which they had done with the Europeans on human rights, in order to deflect attention away from the problem. When the Americans should have been re-engaging with ASEAN, they were preoccupied with the 'war on terror' and the invasion of Iraq. It was during these critical years (2001–05) when America appeared to be absent from Southeast Asia that China rapidly built the necessary political trust with regional governments and backed by economic assistance. ASEAN's secretary general, Rodolfo Severino Jr, pithily stated at the time that 'China is really emerging from this (crisis) smelling good.'[3]

The consequences of American neglect of Southeast Asia became apparent only after 2005. According to one American survey (Congressional Research Service of the US Congress), China's imports from ASEAN grew by a staggering 240 per cent in just five years from US $22.09 billion in 2000 to US $75.01 billion in 2005. In that same period, US imports from ASEAN increased by just 12.5 per cent. China's exports to ASEAN also grew by 220 per cent to US $55.46 billion in the same five-year period, surpassing the US exports which had barely grown by 4.7 per cent to reach US $44.37 billion.[4] Though, in 2005, America was still by far the largest investor, ASEAN's perceptions about America and China were already dramatically changing. Warning bells such as the CRS Report in 2006 were not given adequate attention in Washington. By the time the Americans realized what was happening, and announced their 'pivot to Asia' in 2011, it was possibly too late. Attributing this remarkable transformation entirely to Chinese diplomacy might not be entirely accurate. While China seized the opportunity and quickly crafted a policy that catered to the requirements of ASEAN governments, it was America that gave them the space to do that. America continued to view Southeast Asia very largely from the security perspective. They failed to grasp the fact that, after the end of the Cold War, ASEAN countries no longer needed a heightened American security presence as much as they needed their economic assistance in order to fulfil people's socio-economic expectations and retain legitimacy. By failing to reorient their policy towards Southeast Asia, America ceded ground, as this region fell lower and lower in the American priorities after the collapse of the Soviet Union. The Chinese grasped the new situation and made trade and economy the principal platforms on which to build a post-Cold War relationship with Southeast Asia.

Another region that drew China in was Central Asia. Here, the Russian withdrawal from the region after the Cold War brought challenges for China from the perspective of preserving sovereignty and territorial integrity. China now had to contend with multiple weak nation states on its north-western periphery, adjacent to where China's Muslim population was concentrated. After the fall of the Najibullah government in Afghanistan in 1992, China was fearful that Islamic radicalization in Afghanistan might spill over to the Xinjiang Uyghur Autonomous Region. China had to craft a Central Asian policy that safeguarded its security interests while also bearing in mind that the Russian Federation still regarded itself to be the regional overlord. It adopted a two-pronged approach. Bilaterally, China pushed for the finalization of long-disputed boundaries with the newly independent Central Asian republics, and built trust and confidence to harness the active cooperation of the successor states of the Soviet Union so as to maintain stability in China's periphery.[5] Multilaterally, it was the prime mover behind the setting up of the Shanghai Cooperation Organization (SCO) in 1996. Russia was co-opted in order to dampen doubts that China was expanding its influence at the expense of Russia. The SCO's objective was to pre-empt American influence in this region after the fall of the Soviet Union. The anxiety that China (and Russia) had on this count increased after the Americans established a permanent presence in Afghanistan in 2001. The Chinese viewed the Americans as an external force in the region that might open a new front in the 'containment' of China. China's security policy in Central Asia after 9/11, therefore, doubled down on limiting the spread of American influence. The SCO gathered steam under President Hu Jintao (proposals to include Iran, India and Pakistan pointed in this direction). By the early 2000s, other important factors also came into play, notably trade and energy. From the perspective of trade, China's primary interest was in the transit of goods to Europe and the Middle East through this region. It pursued this objective by opening road and rail transport networks between Xinjiang and the Central Asian republics, by financing infrastructure development, among others. Energy was the other focus of Chinese interest, and Kazakhstan's Aktyubinsk and Uzen oil fields became primary targets for acquisition, to be followed by the building of transboundary pipelines. Thus, the Chinese actively courted the regimes in Central Asia with financing and political support. By 2012, China had forged strong transit, energy and security linkages with several CARs.

Beyond its immediate periphery, the Chinese also began venturing out into more distant parts of the world, especially Africa, a continent of more than one billion souls and teeming with natural resources. European governments and Western corporations had dominated this continent for two centuries until, in the late 1990s, the Chinese began their determined push into this area. One hears two competing narratives about China's presence in Africa. The Western one hews to the view that China's Africa policy is a premeditated and state-directed grand design to control Africa's energy and mineral resources using unfair business practices. The Chinese prefer to believe that their presence in Africa is simply an externalization of their drive to modernize a backward and pre-industrial economy.[6] It is true, China needed a steady supply of raw material for its modernization and that this could only come from

Africa. The question is whether China's 'extractive' behaviour was akin to neo-colonialism.

Prior to 1990, China's Africa policy had been ideologically driven. Political, diplomatic and occasional financial support was given to African liberation movements, revolutionary groups and freedom fighters. China's most tangible contribution was the supply of weapons (according to one report China sold weapons worth US $147 million prior to 1989), and the 1,860 kilometre-long Tanzania–Zambia railway.[7] China had worked at building ties with Africa since the Afro-Asian conference in Bandung in 1955, and this came in handy after the Tiananmen Incident when China was pilloried by the West and the Africans came to China's rescue in international forums. The political objective of denying Taiwan diplomatic space in Africa also gained speed after 1990. But the real outreach to Africa was to come only after the year 2000. It began with China's search for energy.

Until 1993 China had been a net oil exporter. By the early 1990s, the stagnating production at China's onshore oilfields, notably Daqing, made it imperative to secure imported energy. The Middle East was the most obvious source. But in light of the Gulf War and the domination of this region by the Americans, it made sense for the state-owned Chinese oil companies to diversify supplies. China's industrial growth, which was just taking off in the mid-1990s, also compelled state-owned companies to join in the hunt for raw materials and other resources. These largely economic reasons led the Chinese state to encourage the SOEs to look beyond China's borders – the new policy of 'going out' (*zou chu qu*). At that point, most Chinese corporations (overwhelmingly SOEs) lacked the experience in doing international business, but they were hungry and took whatever resources they could grasp.

One Chinese writer described it as hit-and-miss tactics.[8] The Chinese state backed these efforts. This made for adventurous and risky investments by Chinese corporations and even by the Chinese state in troubled regions of Africa. A classic case was Angola, a former Portuguese colony located on the West coast of Africa that had descended into a civil war in 1975 so devastating that few others ventured to do business there despite its vast petroleum and mineral reserves. The end of the civil war in 2002 coincided with China's new *zou chu qu* policy. In 2004, China offered Angola an oil-backed loan of US $2 billion, followed by an additional US $1 billion a year later. This credit line was used by China Petroleum and Chemical Corporation, or SINOPEC, one of world's largest oil refining, gas and petrochemical conglomerates, to acquire stakes in three Angolan oil blocks and was also utilized by Chinese companies to build critical infrastructure, including a 1,300-kilometre railway from the port of Benguela to the interior. In 2006, Premier Wen Jiabao offered an additional US $2 billion as economic assistance. The investments carried high political risk, but China walked away with the rewards. This sort of risky commercial behaviour backed by the Chinese state was repeated throughout Africa, from Sudan to Gabon, and by 2005 China was buying about 38.5 million metric tonnes of crude oil from African fields alone.

China wants the world to think that its activities in Africa flowed solely from economic considerations and was a consequence of its interdependence on and integration with the global economy. However, there were strategic factors at play as well that motivated China's Africa policy. The Chinese Communist Party, especially after 2004, believed that the West could disrupt supplies of strategic resources including oil and gas in order to halt China's rise, and wanted to secure the resource chains to the extent feasible. Since both the SOEs and the policy banks that financed their business ventures overseas were under the complete control of the Party, the new policy allowed them the freedom to do business with African countries of dubious financial standing, such as Angola, Gabon or Sudan, even if this was financially unprofitable or of questionable sustainability. It was the Chinese state that crafted the diplomatic–political narrative that backed Chinese companies in Africa.

Taiwan was also a factor in China's African outreach. Despite the steady attrition in the number of countries that recognized Taiwan as a legitimate government in the 1990s, a sizeable number of governments on the African continent still had ties to it. China saw its economic activity in Africa as also serving the objective of detaching these countries from Taiwan. China used 'grant-and-loan diplomacy' in Africa to compete with Taiwan's 'dollar diplomacy'. Africa became a battleground over which the government represented the real China. In 1998 China secured the big 'prize'. South Africa switched diplomatic recognition from Taiwan to the People's Republic of China. This led to other small African states also switching sides, and once the dominoes began to fall in Beijing's direction, it quickly capitalized on this development and established the Forum for China–Africa Cooperation (FOCAC) in October 2000 to build its continental African strategy. Africa's leadership was systematically wooed. Chinese leaders made it a point to regularly visit the African continent every year whereas leaders from other countries rarely ventured there. China offered substantial loans, many of a commercial nature, with no strings attached, and, in particular, without imposing political conditions or asking for them to comply with Western standards. The West claimed that China's financial support in the troubled parts of

Africa was helping to prop up tyrannical regimes. China said that their presence in Africa was a force for change after decades of economic exploitation by the West and centuries of poverty. In the early part of this century, for many Africans, it certainly looked that way. In January 2006, the State Council issued its white paper on Africa, and later the same year, at the third meeting of FOCAC in November 2006, it declared a strategic partnership with Africa. President Hu Jintao also announced a China–Africa Development Fund of US $5 billion. The result was a massive uptick in China's presence on the continent. America's trade with Africa grew from US $39 billion in the year 2000 to US $113 billion by 2012; in the same period China's trade with Africa went from US $10 billion to US $180 billion. The same was true about arms sales to Africa. The Chinese focus was on small arms trade with low price points; by 2011 China controlled 25 per cent of this market. According to the Stockholm International Peace Research Institute (SIPRI), China provided more than US $2.5 billion in arms to Africa from 2002 to 2010. It is safe to say that by the time the Global Financial Crisis came around, China was a visible presence in every African country and was seen as a viable alternative or option to Western capital and technology.

China's push into Africa was not done by subterfuge. The rest of the world did not necessarily regard China's activities in Africa as harmful to the global order until much later. Nor were their methods very different from what the Europeans had adopted earlier. For example, China's offer of a loan-for-resources deal to Angola or Sudan was also not uniquely a Chinese activity, since the West had also practised this.[9] Where risk or political instability deterred Western companies from sinking funds, the Chinese jumped in. So long as China's activity did not directly impinge on

Western commercial interests in Africa, Western governments appeared to take a benign view, giving China the benefit of the doubt. China took full advantage of that. It scooped up massive resources in the form of long-term arrangements or outright purchases. It was only after China had risen in 2012 that the West began to talk of Chinese exceptionalism in Africa and levelled allegations of them as being self-serving or insincere.

If China pursued resources in Africa, it needed Middle Eastern oil in increasing quantities after 2000 when it became a major energy importer (30 per cent of its energy). It began with President Jiang Zemin's visit to Saudi Arabia in 1999 and the establishment of the 'strategic oil partnership'. Domestic economic requirements may have initially driven the Chinese companies to 'go out' for energy, but the feelings of dependence upon international players (who were primarily Western) and, therefore, a sense of becoming hostage to their geostrategic games, gave Chinese leaders a clear rationale and interest in crafting an energy policy in Hu Jintao's second term that was driven more by strategic interests than by market needs.[10] The American intervention in Iraq in 2003, which the Chinese felt was motivated by American greed to secure the vast Iraqi oil deposits for themselves, heightened Chinese anxieties. The Chinese worked on a dual-problem solving approach – reducing dependence by direct investment in oil fields and reducing transportation risk by building physical infrastructure – ports, pipelines, refining capacities – in order to ensure uninterrupted supply.

The question is whether China's quest for energy was a trojan horse for broader geostrategic objectives. It has to be conceded that China faced genuine energy constraints as its economy boomed after 1995. Its indigenous oil production grew by less than

40 per cent from 138 million metric tonnes in 1990 to 190 million metric tonnes by 2008, while in the same period, its demand went up by 230 per cent, from 100 million metric tonnes in 1990 to 376 million metric tonnes by 2008.[11] So, it can be said that economics was a primary driver behind investments in the Middle East, but it was not the only one. In 2005 a senior member of President Hu Jintao's brain trust, Zheng Bijian, who crafted the phrase 'peaceful rise', had identified and highlighted energy and resource constraints as the top challenge for China in his essay, 'The Rise of China: Three Strategies Coping with Three Challenges,' in the *People's Daily*. Between 1995 and 2006, China's three national oil majors (CNPC, SINOPEC, CNOOC) were already investing in oil fields abroad. According to one estimate, they collectively invested more than US $27 billion in that ten-year period.[12] The scale of the investment suggested that these investments had been authorized by the Chinese state. This was also the time when the Chinese leadership began to look at ways to circumvent the possibility of an American-led blockade of the sea lanes of communication, which was first articulated by Hu Jintao as the 'Malacca dilemma' (*maliujia kunju*). While the Americans basked in the domination of the seas and their control over oil and gas, the Chinese insecurities led them to begin strategic planning for eroding American domination of the sea lanes of communication. There is, then, no doubt that by the mid-2000s, not withstanding Chinese protestations to the contrary, China's energy diplomacy had both a strategic and commercial angle. Yet, those who tended to regard the activities of Chinese national oil companies as strategic actions at the time were termed alarmists.[13] There was the case of CNOOC's efforts to acquire an American oil company, UNOCAL, in June 2005 which ran into Congressional opposition until the deal fell apart. When

CNOOC, whose bid was US $2 billion more than Chevron's, was forced to withdraw, Congress's reaction was described by some as 'hysterical'.[14] Even the odd case of American suspicion of and resistance to Chinese strategic moves was lambasted.

In the Gulf, China focused on the two main players – Saudi Arabia and Iran. Despite the deeply troubled Saudi–Iran relationship, China entered into 'strategic partnerships' with both in 1999 and 2000, respectively. In the case of the Saudis, long-term supply arrangements and cross investments in oilfields and refineries, and in the case of Iran, which was facing sanctions, the doubling of oil imports between 2000 and 2009 and Chinese credit lines and investments in Yadaravan and Garmsar oil fields cemented the relationships. It also helped that by then China had replaced Russia as the primary arms supplier to Iran, helped its missile programme and also sold weapons to the Saudis. Post 9/11 China became a soothing presence in the Gulf and a safe haven for Saudi investment. In July 2004, the six finance ministers of the Gulf Cooperation Council (six Gulf states) signed the Framework Agreement on Economy, Trade, Investment and Technology Cooperation, and agreed to negotiate a free trade zone. Kuwaiti, Saudi and Emirati funds flowed into the building of refining and storage capacities in China. As for Iran, Chinese imports of Iranian oil grew from 1 per cent of total imports in 1990 to nearly 16 per cent by 2006, while trade burgeoned from US $1.2 billion in 1998 to US $8 billion by 2006. On the one hand, the Chinese joined the Americans in sanctioning Iran for its nuclear programme, and on the other, they expanded their bilateral economic ties and skilfully played their relationship with the Iranians to extract concessions from the Americans, allowing them to believe that they were helping America on the nuclear issue and securing their oil and political interests with Iran in return. It is, in retrospect, amazing that one RAND Corporation study concluded that although Beijing took a state-centric view of energy security, there was no 'evidentiary basis' for concluding that it was a state-controlled geostrategic effort,[15] or that its forays in the region were not necessarily a cause for American alarm. It was even suggested that the US might consider encouraging China to become more involved in efforts to improve regional stability.[16] Clear evidence of Chinese strategic intentions, in writings and statements and reinforced by their decision to send PLA flotillas on anti-piracy operations in the Gulf from 2008, was pushed aside, because it was thought that China was pursuing the 'wary dragon' strategy of being a friend to all enemy to none, whereas its real intention was to undermine American hegemony over the control of global energy.

Aside from its bilateral diplomacy in Africa, the Middle East and Central and Southeast Asia, China also took to multilateral diplomacy in a big way during this period. This was the period of American exceptionalism, demonstrated by unilateral US military action in Serbia, Kosovo and Iraq, and it was not liked by many countries who felt vulnerable. China sensed the opportunity to win their support by balancing American unilateralism with its support for multilateralism. It created or joined, among others, the Asia-Pacific Economic Conference (1991), the ASEAN Regional Forum (1994), the Shanghai Cooperation Organization (1996), the Comprehensive Test Ban Treaty or CTBT (1996), the ASEAN+China Dialogue (1996), the Russia–India–China Group (2001) known as RIC, the Six Party Talks on Korea (2003), the East Asia Summit (2005) and BRICS (2006). It entered into free trade agreement negotiations with a wide range of countries – the objectives ranged from market access to strategic reassurances, and was also used to gain commitments from many countries on recognizing China as a 'market economy' under the WTO.

It deployed its growing financial capacity to provide alternate financing for developing countries that did not like Western conditionalities. According to Chinese statistics, outbound investment jumped from less than US $2 billion in 1999 to US $26.5 billion by 2007. Through its diplomatic, economic and cultural efforts, the Chinese were able to divide the West and woo the rest, so that when it was time for them to challenge the West, China was confident that the rest of the world would not line up behind the Americans.

:CHAPTER 5:

The Malacca Dilemma

O N A SNOWY DAY IN JANUARY 1998 XU ZENGPING, A CHINESE businessman based out of Hong Kong, stood on the deck of the *Varyag*, a partially constructed Kuznetsov-class aircraft carrier that was being built by the erstwhile Soviet Union at the Nikoyalev shipyards on the Black Sea, now in Ukraine, before the Soviet Union had collapsed in 1991. The Ukrainians had no money to complete the construction and had, therefore, shopped the carrier around to world governments, including the Chinese, in the hopes of finding a buyer for it. It is believed that a Chinese military delegation had visited Ukraine in 1992 to see this ship, although President Leonid Kravchuk subsequently denied all knowledge of it.[1] There were no other takers. Now, six years later, Xu had apparently bought it for US $20 million and wanted to convert it into a floating casino-cum-hotel anchored off Macao. (Macao, located on China's southern coast close to Hong Kong, had been a Portuguese colony since the mid-sixteenth century, which had legalized gambling since 1962 and was, therefore, a major tourist attraction. The territory finally reverted to China in February 1999.) Xu Zengping set up a shell company in Macao – *Agencia Touristica Diversoes Chong Lot*.[2] He claimed that he had obtained the requisite license to run an offshore casino from the colonial government of Macao, a claim that they subsequently denied. The Stockholm International Peace Research Institute, that publishes the world's leading journal on international arms transfers, later reported that this firm had no licence, no real address and assets of only US $125,000, so it is unclear how it could afford to buy the ship. The report concluded that the *Varyag* had been bought by the PLA Navy for copying its technology.[3] The Hong Kong media similarly reported that Chong Lot, and its parent company – Chin Luck Holdings based in Hong Kong – had close ties to the Chinese People's Liberation Army.[4] Xu, it turned out, had also served in the PLA, and confirmed this many years later. He claims that he was not paid even a fraction of what it had cost him to purchase and sail the *Varyag* from the Ukraine to China.[5]

Xu decided to tow the ship from the Black Sea to China. Turkey controlled the Bosphorus Strait, the only opening from the Black Sea, through which the ship was required to transit. Turkish authorities initially denied permission for the ship's passage. Following prolonged negotiations which took months, it is believed that the Chinese government offered a generous aid and tourism package of US $360 million in return for Turkey's permission for the *Varyag* to transit through the Bosphorus.[6] By March 2002, the ship had made its way to Dalian in north-eastern China. All pretence was dropped once the ship reached Chinese waters. Nobody was surprised that the *Varyag* had bypassed Macao, since its waters are too shallow to berth an aircraft carrier.[7] Dalian is a major shipbuilding centre for PLA naval vessels. Talk about using the *Varyag* as a floating casino ceased and the global strategic community grappled with the idea that China had finally got its hands on an aircraft carrier, albeit moth-eaten, and what that might mean for the Indo-Pacific region.

The Chinese purchase of the *Varyag* was neither impulsive nor whimsical. It was the end result of nearly fifteen years of persistent efforts by the Chinese to develop and acquire carrier technologies. In 1982, Admiral Liu Huaqing had assumed charge of the PLA Navy which was, at the time, an ageing fleet of floating rust buckets that could barely patrol the Chinese coastline. Mao Zedong wanted to build a modern navy with Soviet assistance in 1958. At the time, the Americans posed an existential challenge to the new communist state off the eastern seaboard of China. Mao spoke with Soviet leader Nikita Khrushchev. Disagreement between them over the Soviet demands for joint command over the PLA Navy (PLAN) and the use of Chinese bases in the Pacific led to a tiff between Mao and Khrushchev, and ended Chinese hopes of securing any help from the Soviets.[8] Subsequently, after the Soviets had replaced the Americans as the primary threat to China from the mid-1960s onwards, their focus turned to its land-based forces. China shared a long land border with the erstwhile Soviet Union from where it perceived the most likely threat. Naval modernization receded into the background. Thus, it was only in 1982, when Admiral Liu Huaqing took charge as the commander-in-chief of the PLA Navy, that serious efforts at naval expansion restarted.

China had previously made several efforts to secure a carrier. In the mid-1980s it had made an unsuccessful bid to acquire the Argentine light aircraft carrier – *Vienticinco de Mayo*.[9] China was more successful when its ship-breaking industry managed to buy the ageing Australian carrier – *Melbourne* – in 1985. As it was being dismantled, Chinese naval architects and designers got their first good look at how it had been designed and built. The flight deck was reportedly kept intact for pilot training.[10] Simultaneously, the PLA's '708 Institute' began feasibility studies on aircraft carrier design in a 600-metre model pool in Taihu Lake (Jiangsu province) in the early 1980s.[11] In the 1990s, other opportunities had come along besides the offer from Ukraine. Spain's ship-building company, Empresa Nacional Bazan offered to build a low-cost lightweight carrier (23,000 metric tonne) and France reportedly offered the aircraft carrier *Clemenceau* free of cost to the Chinese if they agreed to award the refurbishment and upgradation contracts to French companies (much like the Russian offer to India for the carrier *Admiral Gorshkov*).[12] Apparently, the Chinese did not wish to spend half a billion dollars on either. The Chinese managed to lay their hands on two more Soviet-era carriers – *Kiev* and *Minsk* – at the turn of the century.[13] Thus, by the time the *Varyag* arrived in Dalian in March 2002, the Chinese had got a close look at three other aircraft carriers, and were in a good position to begin experimenting with the *Varyag*. In order to avoid speculation about their naval plans, the Chinese engaged in obfuscation, claiming as late as in the mid-2000s that China had no intention of building an aircraft carrier. It was only after visuals of the ship undergoing the refit came to light that the Chinese military asserted that it had the right to possess its aircraft carrier.[14] The first official confirmation that the carrier *Varyag* was going to be pressed into naval service came in July 2011, nine years after it had arrived in Dalian. Now renamed the *Liaoning*, she sailed from Dalian in August 2011 for her maiden sea trial.[15] It was commissioned into the PLA Navy in September 2012.

The *Varyag*'s acquisition marked the start of China's indigenous carrier-building programme and also the beginning of doctrinal shifts in Chinese naval planning. The doctrinal shift was also driven by Chinese Admiral Liu Huaqing who believed that the Pacific Century was going to be China's, and that Chinese sea power would become increasingly critical in guaranteeing China's sovereignty and control over the near seas and protecting its maritime rights and interests. These objectives, in his view, could only be secured when China exercised 'sea control' over the two island chains, which were dominated by the American navy after the end of the Second World War and allowed the Americans to throttle attempts by the PLA Navy from breaking out into the Western Pacific. The first of these island chains ran from the Japanese archipelago and the Ryuku islands to Taiwan and the Philippines; the second originated in Japan's Ogasawara-Guntō (Bonin) islands and extended to the Marianas and the western Caroline islands. The task that Admiral Liu set for the PLA Navy was to break out of these two island chains into the blue ocean.[16] The acquisition of the *Varyag* was central to this Chinese naval strategy. The long pursuit for carrier technology is a good example of how the Chinese systematically, and in a deliberate fashion, met their strategic requirements by first securing the know-how and doing their research, before they executed their naval expansion plans. They stayed below the radar and almost never revealed their true intentions.

In the interim, while the PLA Navy was scaling up to fulfil its new role, the Chinese began to systematically construct the historical, legal and factual grounds to lay claim to island territories in the South and East China Seas. In 1992, the National People's Congress passed the Law on Territorial Seas and Contiguous Zones. This law claimed the entire set of South China Sea islands – the Pratas (Dongsha), the Paracel (Xisha) and the Spratly (Nansha) island groups, collectively known in China as Nanhai Zhudao – as sovereign Chinese territory. This reinforced the earlier claim promulgated in 1958, called the Declaration of the Government of the People's Republic of China on China's Territorial Seas. This new law also asked foreign navies to seek prior permission for the innocent passage of any foreign warship that desired to transit through the South China Sea*.[17] In 1998, China passed the Law on Exclusive Economic Zone and Continental Shelf of the PRC, giving additional maritime rights beyond the 1992 law.

Even as this legislation was being enacted, Chinese historians began to create new historical facts in support of China's extended jurisdictional and territorial claims over the seas surrounding China. They claimed that the 'islands'** of the South China Sea (Nanhai Zhudao) had been an integral part of Chinese territory for centuries. Chinese seafarers had discovered them as early as the second century BCE. Historical records going back to the Eastern Han dynasty (25–200 CE), containing geographical locations and geomorphologic conditions of the islands, were cited as evidence in support of this claim. The Song dynasty (960–1279 CE) had, as per the Chinese claim, even appointed an Imperial Envoy for

---

* Article 19 of the United Nations Convention on Law of the Sea (UNCLOS) provides 'right of innocent passage' to warships for purposes of traversing the territorial seas so long as it is continuous and expeditious, and so long as it is not prejudicial to the peace, good order and security of the coastal state. However, the 1992 law adopted by China made such right of innocent passage conditional upon the approval of the Chinese authorities. This position was reiterated when China ratified UNCLOS in July 1996.

** In many cases, these are not officially recognized by the UNCLOS as actual islands, because they fall short of the requirements defined in the International Convention on Law of the Sea. China, on the other hand, insists on calling them islands because this allows them to claim an exclusive economic zone around each of the 'islands'.

Management and Pacification to govern these southern territories. The islands were depicted as part of the Chinese Empire on the official maps of the Qing dynasty (1644–1911). China also pointed to the establishment by the Nationalist Government, in March 1947, of the Taiping Dao Nansha Qundao Office of Administration under the Guangdong provincial control as proof that China had for long administered the islands.[18] None of these claims were based on treaties or agreements with other parties or claimants. The Chinese simply expected the international community to accept them as valid in terms of international law because they had seemingly met the requirements of 'acquisition by discovery'.[19] On the other hand, they turned their argument on its head when they rejected territorial claims by others, including India, on similar grounds by stating that these were unacceptable because the concerned country had not provided any treaty basis in support of such claims. This is a good example of how China applied double standards in its international dealings depending on whether it is the claimant or the aggressor party. The question of principle, seemingly, is merely a matter of convenience, to be used or discarded in order to fit their narrative.

Along with the passing of laws and the invention of 'historical' claims to sovereignty and jurisdiction over the South China Sea, China commenced what has been aptly described as a policy of 'creeping assertiveness' on the seas. Their tactic was to establish a steadily expanding physical presence in the South China Sea without provoking a military confrontation.[20] In July 1992, China occupied the Da Lac reef claimed by Vietnam. In February 1995, Chinese structures began to appear on the Philippines' Mischief Reef. In 1999–2000, Chinese fishing boats began to establish claims over Scarborough shoal in the Macclesfield Bank, which was claimed by the Philippines. This was paired with China's aggressive behaviour towards Taiwan in 1995–96 when it conducted missile tests in the Taiwan Straits (ostensibly because Taiwan was having its first free general election in which a pro-independence leader, Lee Teng-hui, was elected as president). It was only a matter of time before their behaviour aroused concern among the ASEAN claimant states. China was not perturbed with their expressions of concerns, per se. Their real concern was with the possibility of American involvement and intervention, because its naval power was no match for the American seventh fleet. Therefore, China changed tack by adopting a policy that was 'outwardly soft and inwardly hard.'[21] This meant that, at least outwardly, the Chinese appeared to adopt a more reasonable posture on the South China Sea issue and offered to negotiate with other claimant states. They cleverly suggested that such negotiations had to be bilateral, that is, with individual claimant states and not with ASEAN as a group or with outside parties. They did not want the issue to become regionalized or multi-lateralized or to risk American interference on jurisdictional and territorial questions.[22] To deflect attention from their longer-term goals which were really to get full control over the South China Sea, they additionally sought to allay the concerns of the ASEAN countries as a group by agreeing on a Declaration of Code of Conduct (DOC) of parties in the South China Sea with ASEAN. (ASEAN's concerns over Chinese assertiveness in the South China Sea had led them to collectively endorse the idea of having a regional code of conduct, to deter further Chinese encroachments after China's occupation of the Mischief Reef in 1996.) China was thus able to blunt a united front on the South China Sea territorial dispute and keep the Americans at bay.

Inwardly, the Chinese position remained both hard and unyielding. They had no intentions of allowing the negotiations on the DOC to tie their hands in any manner. The Chinese ensured that the declaration that they signed with ASEAN on 4 November 2002 was neither legally binding nor enforceable. China never spelt out its commitments under the DOC. It referred to the 'shelving of disputes', yet nowhere in the document did China define the scope and nature of these disputes.[23] Since China had already claimed all the island territories under domestic law from 1992 onwards, by inference, when China agreed in the DOC to the mutual delimitation of each other's maritime jurisdictions, what it meant to say was that other claimants should accept all of China's territorial claims in the South China Sea. The rest of the offerings – joint development of resources, joint marine scientific research and the CBMs, or confidence building measures for joint consultation and resolution of differences – were mere window-dressing to mollify ASEAN, prevent a common American–ASEAN approach in the South China Sea and hide China's 'creeping expansionism.' If the relevant parties in Southeast Asia realized the irony of it, they did not choose to call out the Chinese publicly.

By the mid-2000s, after having set their naval expansion plans into motion and laid the basis for their claims to the South China Sea, the Chinese prepared to tackle a fast-emerging strategic concern. The new concern had arisen because of China's remarkable economic development over the past ten years which, by 2003, had made it a global trading and business nation. One reason for the rapid pace at which China had moved from being a near-autarkic economy to becoming an integral part of the global economy was due to the freedoms that it enjoyed on the high seas. Given the growing significance of the high seas for the future growth of the Chinese economy, the task of keeping the sea lanes of communication open and secure for Chinese trade and energy supplies assumed critical importance by the end of the 1990s. It was, therefore, to be expected that Chinese strategists would begin to fret over the sea-denial capabilities of the Americans and their allies, and seek to neutralize these risks in geographies that China regarded as crucial to its overall national security and economic well-being. The Chinese are obsessed with one waterway, in particular – the Straits of Malacca. In order to understand the importance of this particular waterway, it is necessary to briefly recount the historical role of China in Southeast Asia.

China has traditionally considered the entire Southeast Asia as falling within its sphere of influence. They regard the colonization of the region by the Western powers as a historical aberration, and the Americans as interlopers. The rewriting of Asia's history by the West has largely erased from public memory the maritime history of China, which, together with India, were important maritime countries for centuries before the Europeans arrived in the Indo-Pacific region. Due to their (India and China) maritime trade in the Indo-Pacific, they accounted for over half the global GDP circa 1700.[24] China had had important trading relationships with Southeast Asian kingdoms since the fifth century CE. Over time, this had evolved into more formal tributary relationships between the seventh and twelfth centuries CE.[25] Chinese overlordship in Southeast Asia reached its apogee during the early Ming dynasty. From 1405 to 1433, the Ming Emperor Yong Le projected Chinese imperial power in a series of maritime voyages led by Admiral Zheng He that sailed into the Indian Ocean. The Chinese were not interested in establishing the Western kind of hegemony, but instead in imposing a Chinese world order in which it would be recognized universally as the supreme power, in exchange for guaranteeing the legitimacy and security of the Southeast Asian kingdoms. In other words, a looser form of imperial control.

One area, historically speaking, which the Chinese Empire had been especially interested in was the Strait of Malacca, which was dominated by the port of Melaka (Malacca) on the west coast of the Malay peninsula. Whoever controlled this port could ensure safe transit for merchant shipping through the vital Malacca Strait. The Malacca Strait is a 500-nautical-miles-long sea corridor of relatively shallow waters and just 11 miles wide at its narrowest point, located at one end between the eastern coast of Sumatra and the western coast of Malaysia and joined at the other end by the Singapore Strait. It is the shortest passage between the Indian Ocean and the South China Sea. China, therefore, took a special interest in this Southeast Asian kingdom. In 1405, they accorded their formal recognition to its ruler, Parmeswara, a Sumatran Hindu prince who converted to Islam and became the first Islamic Sultan on the Malay peninsula. In exchange for accepting Chinese overlordship, the Chinese channelized trade through Melaka, eventually allowing it to surpass the Srivijayan Empire's port at Palembang as the leading regional trading hub.[26] With the backing of China and under Chinese naval protection, Melaka quickly became the principal entrepôt between the Indian and Pacific oceans.[27] History might have been rather different if the Chinese (and Indian) rulers had continued with their maritime activities, but both turned inwards to focus on their land borders from the mid-fifteenth century. With the eclipse of Chinese sea power after the mid-fifteenth century, and the subsequent seizure of Melaka by the Portuguese in 1511, Melaka became for the Chinese just another small town on the Malay peninsula. That is, until 2003.

In November 2003 (at the Party Central Economic Work Conference), President Hu Jintao declared that 'certain major powers' (unnamed) were bent on controlling the Malacca Strait, and called for the adoption of new strategies to mitigate this perceived vulnerability. President Hu Jintao's reference to China's 'Malacca Strait Dilemma' (*maliujia kunju*) returned the maritime issue to the front and centre of Chinese geostrategic policy after four centuries. Prima facie what seemed to be driving Chinese concerns was the possible interdiction of vital energy supplies from the Gulf and resources from Africa, which were necessary to power the expanding Chinese economy.[28] By 1993, China was running out of its oil. A decade later, in 2004, China's energy consumption had grown so exponentially that it needed to import close to 40 per cent of its annual requirement. According to one estimate, China doubled its oil imports between 1999 and 2002.[29] Chinese leaders began to focus on the critical connection between China's energy security and its national security. More significantly, the leadership felt that their plans for China's transformation may not succeed without enough energy, as well as the uninterrupted flow of raw materials, to fuel the Chinese economy. They feared that unless they could keep the economic engine ticking, the legitimacy of the Chinese Communist Party might at some point fall into doubt. Thus, national security concerns and the Party's concerns about its legitimacy seemingly converged on 'one lane' – the Strait of Malacca. It came to be viewed as the one 'must secure' point from both perspectives. Hu Jintao's reference to the 'Malacca Dilemma' reflected the depth of this national worry and obsession. Hence, the Straits of Malacca became the key factor in the shaping of China's maritime strategy.[30]

There were other challenges, of course, for China to confront, such as maritime piracy in the South China Sea. According to one account, there were 1,220 actual or attempted cases of hijacking of vessels between 1995 and 2005. This led the regional countries – Singapore, Malaysia, Indonesia and Thailand – to begin joint patrols.[31] The Chinese also had to plan for the potential closure of the strait to prevent the disruption to shipping as a result of possible acts of maritime terrorism, especially against oil tankers, which had become a real possibility after 9/11 because of the presence of Islamic radical elements, including Al Qaeda affiliates, in parts of Southeast Asia.[32] A single oil tanker that sank in the narrower parts of the Malacca Strait had the potential to block the channel, with serious consequences for all economies of the region. However, what worried the Chinese the most was the apprehension of access denial. The Americans had the capability to do that.

This concern was exacerbated for Chinese security planners by the steadily improving American relationship with India. Since the 1990s, Chinese military writings had pointed to the strategic location of India's Andaman and Nicobar Islands, and the possibility of it being used in the future to interdict Chinese shipping. Their worst-case scenario was the possibility of a combined US–India naval blockade of the western entrance to the Malacca Strait, and this futuristic scenario acted as a powerful catalyst to the Chinese acquisition of naval power. China commenced a frenzied warship building programme in the mid-2000s and advanced its aircraft carrier ambitions, even as it projected a more benign and accommodating image about itself in the Southeast Asian region in order to allay the concerns of regional players.[33] Chinese diplomats were pressed into service to manage ASEAN's concerns over Chinese naval expansion and to offer economic inducements. At the international level, the Chinese worked to deceive the Americans that China's maritime interests were limited to the near seas, and that it was not their intention to challenge the American supremacy or US alliances in the Pacific. The Hu Jintao administration was able to buy time and space to develop the requisite naval power that would allow the Chinese to progressively enhance their sea control over the South China Sea by 2012. It also allowed them to develop the sort of capabilities that eventually made it much harder, if not virtually impossible, for any other nation to interdict the Chinese navy in the seas surrounding China. China's diplomacy on the South China Sea between 2002 and 2010 must rank as amongst the more sophisticated displays of foreign and national security policy by any country in very recent times.

Aside from the United States, which was the country of primary concern, the Indian Navy was also a subject of Chinese military interest. Chinese maritime scholars looked at India as a potentially strong maritime nation in the twenty-first century, with a strategic advantage in the Indian Ocean. Chinese military publications would regularly level the allegation that India had always regarded the Indian Ocean as its backwater and would at some point 'jump out of the South Asian bathtub to control the Indian Ocean'.[34] The more extreme Chinese views tended to portray India as an inimical power that might try to deny China entry into the Indian Ocean by blocking the western exit to the Strait.[35] The Chinese were quite aware that the Indian Navy, in the early 2000s, still lacked the capacity to interdict Chinese shipping at the north-western end of the Malacca Strait. India had never tried to secure absolute sea-control in the Bay of Bengal nor denied free passage to Chinese maritime traffic. Therefore, such PLA narratives appeared to be more of a convenient justification for China to explain its naval activities in India's maritime neighbourhood, which steadily grew between 2004 and 2014. In order not to raise any alarm in Indian strategic circles, China's policy was what some Chinese strategic analysts called a policy of 'cooperation at the forefront and slow penetration'. The Chinese focused on passive naval exchanges, port building, hydrographic surveys and other such activities that they could claim were non-threatening to the regional balance. They consciously reduced the military colour of their activities in the Indian Ocean, including their port-building ventures (also

JIANG ZEMIN: Plucked from relative obscurity to assume top positions in China, Jiang held the Chinese Communist Party and country together after Deng's death through the early reform period in the 1990s.

HU JINTAO: Colourless and dour in comparison to Jiang Zemin, his inscrutable demeanour and seemingly mild manner belied his steely resolve to ready the Chinese nation to act as a great power.

DENG XIAOPING: The architect of Modern China. His final contribution was to steer a steady course for the Communist Party of China after the fall of European communism in 1990.

WEN JIABAO: He was with Zhao Ziyang in Tiananmen Square hours before Zhao was purged. He succeeded Zhu Rongji and carried through the reforms instituted by him to their logical conclusion.

ZHU RONGJI: The dynamic and no-nonsense premier who staked his political career to make bold reforms that would release the forces of great change and transform the Chinese economy within a decade.

PRESIDENTS CLINTON AND JIANG ZEMIN: Less than five years after Clinton had chided his predecessor for 'coddling dictators', Jiang Zemin's charm offensive in 1997 led to optimism on both sides that this would be the defining partnership of the 21st century.

RAJIV GANDHI AND DENG XIAOPING: Despite their 40-year age difference, they crafted a modus vivendi that stood for 25 years.

A.B. VAJPAYEE AND JIANG ZEMIN: After India's nuclear tests, Vajpayee adroitly repaired the relationship and his 2003 visit to China led to a new initiative to resolve the boundary question with China.

DR MANMOHAN SINGH AND WEN JIABAO: Wen's visit to India in April 2005 marked the most optimistic point in the relationship following the signing of a landmark agreement on guidelines and principles to resolve the boundary issue.

PUDONG, 1992: Mostly open land on the east bank of the Huangpu river, it would establish a special economic zone in 1993 that would become the envy of the world in less than two decades.

PUDONG, 2010: This is the image that is seen most often across the world to mark the coming of age of China as a global power.

THE *VARYAG*: The Russian-Ukrainian aircraft carrier that China bought in the late 1990s as the nucleus of its blue-water navy. Renamed the *Liaoning*, it symbolized new China's power and place in the new century.

THE MALACCA DILEMMA

known as the 'string of pearls') by emphasizing the civilian and developmental aspects and downplaying the dual-use nature of their projects.[36] As a result, the Chinese were able to make significant inroads into the Indian Ocean region until 2012 without overstimulating India's nerves.

China's careful military planning and skilful diplomacy was one reason for its success in building a modern navy during the period 1990–2012. The other part was the lack of ability by other countries to accurately read Chinese intentions. Adequate information about Chinese activities was available to foreign governments. It was known, for instance, that at an enlarged Central Military Commission conference on 24 December 2004, President Hu Jintao had entrusted the PLA (including the navy) with the mandate of safeguarding global peace. Two years later, on 27 December 2006, Hu referred to China as a 'great maritime power' and explicitly called on the PLAN to build a blue-water capability. The same year, a Chinese white paper on defence iterated that the navy would strive for gradual extension of strategic depth for offshore defensive operations, and a subsequent white paper in 2008 extended the navy's role to the conduct of operations in distant waters.[37] The purchase of the *Varyag* had also alerted the Americans to the possibility that the Chinese might be preparing for a range of different missions. On 6 March 2007, a PLA lieutenant general revealed that the carrier project was proceeding smoothly, and this was subsequently confirmed by Zhang Yu, minister-in-charge of the Commission on Science, Technology, and Industry for National Defence (COSTIND).[38] A Chinese admiral, Yin Zhuo, had even spoken of the need for China to have an overseas base. The statement was subsequently retracted but it spoke to Chinese intentions.[39] Thus, by 2008, the rest of the world had substantial information about Chinese naval plans. Based on this information, one perceptive American analyst projected that by 2016–17 the Chinese navy would be able to extend hegemonic leverage in maritime East Asia.[40] But the majority view still seemed to be that the acquisition of a carrier did not necessarily signal a fundamental shift towards the building of a blue-water navy by China. They continued to highlight Chinese inadequacies in C4ISR* and the lack of logistics was a serious constraint on the development of Chinese naval power. Chinese activism in the Spratly Islands was justified in some quarters as a rationale for naval modernization but not necessarily as a change in Chinese policy.[41] Sometimes history was also cited by Western scholars in order to cast doubts over China's ambitious naval plans. Western writings claimed that China had historically always been a land power. It was presumed that simply because China had not pursued a major colonizing effort or tried to establish a true empire in Southeast Asia (like the Europeans), it lacked a maritime tradition.[42] China's references to its historically having been a maritime nation in public documents were dismissed as mere talk and as a departure from China's 'continental' military tradition. It was forgotten that China had been a maritime nation in centuries past.[43] It was only towards the end of the first decade of the twenty-first century that people began to focus on Chinese naval activities, and this was the result of two important developments. First, the Chinese began deploying their warships on anti-piracy missions off the Somali coast in December 2008. By doing this, the Chinese demonstrated a new capability for mounting and sustaining naval expeditions in distant waters. Second, the Chinese navy interdicted the American intelligence-gathering ship – the USNS *Impeccable* –

---

* C4ISR denotes command, control, communications, computers, intelligence, surveillance and reconnaissance.

off the coast of Hainan Island in March 2009. In doing so, they also signalled their readiness to deploy a more assertive posture towards foreign navies that might act in a belligerent manner in the seas surrounding China, including the United States Navy. By the time of the *Impeccable* incident, Beijing's long-term naval planning and development had gained sufficient momentum, so that they could be publicly spelt out by Admiral Wu Shengli, the chief of the PLA Navy. In an interview to Central Chinese Television shortly before the naval review in Qingdao (April 2009), he declared that the PLAN was proceeding to place preparations for maritime military struggle on top of the national security and military strategy based on new naval technologies.[44] It was only then that the global strategic community began to seriously look at the implications of Chinese naval expansion for the Indo-Pacific region.

This rapidly changing landscape of China's maritime interests, objectives and capabilities in the short space of twenty years was reflective of the more fundamental shifts that were simultaneously placed on other matters relating to national defence and the PLA's role in the new century. Deng's great achievement had been to remove the military's direct influence from politics and to reduce the size of the armed forces in order to lessen the burden on the exchequer. Modernization of the armed forces was, however, begun by his two successors. There were two triggers for this. The first was the collapse of the Soviet Union. The United States became the globally dominant power. The international order underwent fundamental changes that China had to adjust to. Given the fact that China was now the world's largest communist state, the Party felt more vulnerable and felt the need to develop the military as part of its larger plans to grow its national power. The second was the sense of shock and awe in the Chinese leadership that was created by the US military action in the Gulf War of 1991. The display of long-range American air and naval power and their capacity to organize a global military alliance against Saddam Hussain in such a short period, which forced him to withdraw from Kuwait without requiring the deployment of US ground forces in significant numbers, made the Chinese PLA realize how backward it really was in terms of both technology and training. It thus brought home the extent of their weakness and outdatedness in modern warfare. These developments spurred Chinese leadership into action.

In January 1993, Jiang Zemin jump-started the transformation in military affairs by announcing the revamped 'Military Strategic Guidelines for the New Period' at an expanded meeting of the Central Military Commission, based on the revised assessment of China's security environment and the changing nature of modern warfare. He pressed for greater professionalization of the PLA, worked to reduce their involvement in commercial businesses, established a new Commission of Science, Technology, and Industry for National Defence (COSTIND) under the State Council that would coordinate foreign arms procurement and indigenous technology development, and focused resources on a limited number of military R&D programmes that would help the PLA to 'leapfrog' (*kuayue wu fazhan*) into the twenty-first century. Since all the defence contractors were SOEs, the decision-making was top-down, and specific weapons that were deemed to be a national priority received funding and backing. Under Jiang and his successor, Chinese defence spending emerged from two decades of stagnation with the infusion of significant funds which, according to one estimate, grew from US $25.30 billion in 1995 to US $153.10 billion by 2012.[45] Jiang also allowed the PLA to patronize defence industries as alternative sources of income through commercial weapons sales, to compensate for their exit from purely civilian commercial enterprises. The question of how to access modern and state-of-the-art foreign technology was more difficult for Jiang because the United States had imposed blanket military sanctions on China after 1989, and had also made the Europeans toe this line. In the 1990s, the Chinese had found ways to access Russian and Israeli technologies, which they were able to integrate into their indigenous production lines.[46] In the 1990s, they began to look for dual-use technologies not covered specifically by American sanctions that the Chinese defence industry could absorb into their manufacturing processes. Under Jiang's successor, the Chinese would find even more innovative ways to bypass the Western sanctions by using the international financial system and the business lobbies to dilute the impact of technology sanctions. And that was not all. China also illegally copied or stole foreign military technologies, including Russian aircraft engines and fighter aircraft technologies. It engaged in cyber-espionage as well. By the time Hu Jintao succeeded Jiang Zemin as the chairman of the Central Military Commission in 2004, due to the latter's military reforms, the face of the Chinese defence industry was rapidly modernizing in significant ways, including in terms of R&D and integration of indigenous technologies. By one estimate, national R&D spending went from US $16.8 billion in 1995 to US $275.3 billion by 2012.[47] All of it may not have been defence-related spending, but in the absence of reliable and transparent data, it should be presumed that China spends more on defence R&D than any country besides the United States.

Jiang Zemin's successor, Hu Jintao, inherited a military that had begun to reform and develop modern military platforms. Hu Jintao's tenure would be notable for the doctrinal changes that happened. The most notable among them was his address to the expanded Central Military Commission, reportedly in December 2004, where he introduced the concept of 'Historic Missions for the PLA in the New Stage of the New Century' or, simply called 'historic missions'.[48] This came to be known later as the 'Three Provides and One Role' decree.[49] The PLA was entrusted with the missions of providing security for the party's rule in China, providing security for China's national development in a strategic period and securing China's sovereignty and territorial integrity. Its most significant element, however, was the 'one role' that Hu allocated to the PLA. By stating that the PLA would have a global role in maintaining world peace and order, Hu Jintao gave the green light to the PLA to perform tasks beyond Chinese homeland defence that it had never envisaged in the first half of the century of communist rule. It was this directive that would lead to China's breakthrough efforts to become the dominant naval power in the Indo-Pacific. This might not have been obvious at the time because of the secrecy under which the party operated, and it was only in 2012, as Hu was stepping down from high office, that he publicly called for China to become a global maritime power, but it was under his eight-year watch as chairman of the Central Military Commission (CMC) that China built the military foundations for its global role. This was not Hu's only achievement. In 2008, the CMC also issued new guidelines for joint training, known as the 'Outline for Military Training and Exercising', calling for actual troops, real equipment and live ammunition drills in place of tabletop exercises and classroom drills, in a serious attempt to prepare the PLA for future combat roles.[50]

In a report for the US–China Economic and Security Commission in 2009, noted China expert James Mulvenon[51] concluded that since 1998 China's defence industries underwent a significant transformation as a result of the policies of Jiang and Hu, making notable advances in areas like missiles, shipbuilding and defence electronics. How was it that China was able to secure access to state-of-the-art technologies from the West even though there were official sanctions in place? Four factors contributed to this process – more money, commercialization of weapons sales, competition between the domestic defence contractors and, most interestingly, the integration of China's defence–industrial complex into global R&D and financial chains, which gave them access to foreign technology, capital and know-how. Mulvenon identified three channels through which China circumvented the Western sanctions – collaborative training with Western companies, creation of joint ventures in the civilian industry with potential dual-use applications and strategic partnerships with Western companies through which they obtained resources and information. For instance, between 1993 and 2008, Boeing trained 37,000 engineers and technicians in facilities established in China. The manufacture of aircraft components in China by Boeing and Airbus industries facilitated technology transfers. In the electronics sector, a Rand Corporation study in 2005 showed how Ericsson, Microsoft and others had transferred core technologies in exchange for gaining market share. Western companies partnered with Chinese companies in the electronics, nuclear energy and outer space areas through joint ventures and technology tie-ups, despite the potential hazards of transferring sanctioned technologies to China. Western corporations that were eager for potentially huge opportunities in the Chinese electronics, nuclear energy or aerospace businesses would work to shape their governments' export control policies around dual-use and sensitive technologies, which would then allow them to enter into joint ventures with the Chinese. As a result, the Chinese were able to access technologies in these key sectors through their Western joint venture partners despite the sanctions. European governments, too, in some cases, pushed for the relaxation of sanctions themselves or looked the other way when their companies secured major contracts. It is also telling that in Mulvenon's report there are several examples of how Chinese defence contractors were able to list their subsidiaries in the Shanghai, Shenzhen and Hong Kong stock exchanges and raise international capital, which helped not only in the development of civilian industries but also in the development of new weapons systems. As a result of methods which were sometimes questionable, and at times with the connivance of their Western partners, by 2012, the Chinese defence industry was on the cusp of significant defence indigenization and dependency on foreign sources was greatly reduced for the most part.

During the first decade of the twenty-first century, one important, and rather disturbing, development for the Chinese was the formation of a nascent quadrilateral grouping between the United States, Japan, India and Australia, colloquially known as the QUAD. The grouping itself was tentative and exploratory in nature but the Chinese reaction was shrill and vociferous, which was surprising. The Chinese declared the QUAD grouping to be a precursor to the formation of an 'Asian NATO' like arrangement that seemed intent on building a coalition of naval powers in the Indo-Pacific to confine China within the first and second island chains.[52] Though some Chinese commentators conceded that the idea of the QUAD amounted to nothing more than an 'armchair strategy' at that point, they were focused on its potential capability to change the geostrategic patterns in the Asia-Pacific and to bring strategic pressure on China. Therefore, the Chinese tried their best to strangle the idea of the QUAD at its inception.[53] The Chinese cited the US Quadrennial Defence Review 2006, in which China was identified as a potential future problem for the United States in the Pacific theatre, as a clear pointer to American intentions. General Luo Yuan, deputy director general of the PLA's World

Military Department at the Academy of Military Sciences, was reported to have said that America wanted to use India, Japan and others in the region to constrain China.[54] China also pointed to the Agreement on Indo-Japanese Defence and Security Cooperation, and the first US–Japan–Australia trilateral strategic dialogue in 2006, the first joint naval exercise between Japan, India and the US off the Japanese coast in 2007, and the low-key functional level discussions in Manila in May 2007 between representatives of the four countries (US, Japan, India and Australia) as some of the building blocks of the 'containment of China' strategy in the making by the US since the mid-2000s. China justified its naval build up in the Indo-Pacific as a counter-response to this development. Given the Chinese argument, it is important to explore the question in greater detail.

It is true that a number of developments were taking place in the Indo-Pacific region at the beginning of the twenty-first century. This was partly because of the wars in Iraq and against terrorism in Afghanistan, and partly due to the vibrant economic growth. The sea lanes of communication, from the Bab El-Mandeb and the Strait of Hormuz in the western Indian Ocean through to the Malacca Strait in the eastern part of the Indian Ocean, through which a substantial amount of energy and trade began to pass, consequently gained in importance. It was only natural that countries with a stake in ensuring the security of economic activity and transportation routes would look at ways and means to strengthen security in the region, including with partners. China's own commercial and naval activity in the Indian Ocean region after the year 2000 had significantly increased for the same reasons. The various bilateral or multilateral arrangements that countries were working out did not automatically mean that they were aimed at any third parties. That is, however, how China tried to portray it. The real question is why China tried to do that. The most likely explanation for the strong Chinese reaction to the initial formation of the QUAD is that the Chinese were fearful that its formation might prematurely expose their naval expansion plans. A substantial part of these plans had already been set into motion in the late 1990s. Hu Jintao's references to the Malacca Dilemma in 2003 would suggest that the Chinese preparations for naval countermeasures against a possible blockade of the Malacca Strait were already well underway. The 'historic missions' mandate given to PLAN in 2004 also represented a major doctrinal shift that pointed to greater Chinese naval activism. The Chinese were hoping that while America was distracted by the war on terror, the nuclear imbroglios with North Korea and Iran and the emerging problems with Putin's Russia, China would have the time to build up naval forces in the Pacific without attracting America's undue attention. The formation of QUAD, which was a specifically Indo-Pacific maritime initiative, threatened to upend these carefully laid Chinese plans. This would explain why the Chinese reacted so strongly to an idea which was still in its formative phase. The label 'Asian NATO' was consciously selected by the Chinese for the four-party grouping in order to cause the greatest possible anxiety among the regional countries. For countries in East Asia that had enjoyed an unprecedented period of prosperity and peace, thanks to the twin benefits of US security guarantees and Chinese economic opportunities, a potentially new Cold War involving its two most important partners was too awful to contemplate. The Chinese exploited these fears in the region, pitting their efforts at all-directional diplomacy, which they said would be benign and beneficial to regional stability and prosperity, with the formation of the QUAD, which they claimed would be inherently destabilizing, because it was a 'club' hostile to China. When QUAD 1.0 was shortlived (for reasons that had nothing to do with the Chinese and more the result of internal rethinking about its purpose), the Chinese breathed a sigh of relief. But they conveniently continued to use it as a cover to legitimize and validate their own naval build up. Regional concerns about the Chinese naval build up were handled through clever diplomacy by senior Chinese diplomats like Yang Jiechi, who took pains to dispel any such concerns by insisting that China's development has been fundamentally peaceful in nature and did not pose a threat to others.[55] Fifteen years down the road, such claims ring hollow and stand at odds with Chinese actions in the South China Sea and the Western Pacific.

Whichever way you look at it, it was in these twenty years, between Deng Xiaoping and Xi Jinping, that China was able to lay the solid foundations for a strong military. That it did so despite the backward state of PLA capacities, the defence–industrial complex in 1989 and the formal military sanctions imposed by the Americans after the Tiananmen Incident shows the sophistication with which the Communist Party of China managed the situation. For the most part, this military expansion remained hidden in the open, partly the result of Chinese deception, but also because the world preferred to take repeated Chinese assurances that they would never seek hegemony or threaten peace and stability. Under the stewardship of general secretaries Jiang Zemin and Hu Jintao, China managed to build the modern military force that has allowed Xi Jinping to challenge the Americans for regional hegemony today. The story about China's Malacca Dilemma is intended to illustrate how important it is to watch what China does over time and to never take the assurances they give at face value.

:CHAPTER 6:

The Party Means Business

On 6 February 2012, Wang Lijun, the police chief of Chongqing (a large city in south-western China with a population of 30 million), which along with the cities of Beijing, Shanghai and Tianjin enjoys the status of a province in China, sought asylum in the American consulate in Chengdu (300 kilometres from Chongqing). The request for asylum was refused by the Americans after twenty-four hours, apparently because a senior Chinese leader, Vice President Xi Jinping, was due to visit the United States. Wang was quietly spirited away to Beijing by China's security agencies. When the facts came to light, they exposed the rot and sleaze beneath the razzle-dazzle of the Chinese economic miracle, and roiled the Chinese Communist Party as possibly no other event has since 1989. It came to be known as the 'Bo Xilai affair'.

Bo Xilai was the party secretary of Chongqing.[1] Handsome, charismatic and flamboyant were some of the words that came to the minds of people who met him. He had impeccable revolutionary credentials. His father, Bo Yibo, a compatriot of Mao and Deng, was counted amongst the 'eight immortals'.² He was, thus, a 'red prince' and there is nothing better in China than to be born one. This meant that he was educated at the best schools and socialized with the children of other communist leaders. These early connections would help him to vault over the heads of ordinary members of the Chinese Communist Party into positions of power at an early age. A fast track inside the Party meant that he could cultivate his support base by enticing or inducing ordinary Party members to hitch themselves to his star in return for significant benefits. And Bo Xilai was undoubtedly one of the brightest stars of the 2000s. He had not only impressed his bosses with his developmental work as mayor of Dalian City (1993–2001) and as governor of Liaoning province (2001–04), but had equally impressed foreign businessmen with his charm and fluency in the English language when he was China's commerce minister from 2004 to 2007. By 2007, he had reached the higher rungs of great power – he was appointed to the Politburo of the Chinese Communist Party and simultaneously sent to Chongqing as the party secretary. Lesser men might have quailed at the enormity of the challenge that confronted him in Chongqing. It ranked twenty-sixth among China's thirty-one provinces in terms of GDP growth, it was heavily polluted, wracked by urban crime and had been neglected in comparison with Shanghai, Guangzhou and Tianjin, which had benefitted from their coastal locations. Bo, however, accepted the challenge with gusto.

Combining state-funded infrastructure growth with his clever positioning of the city as a low-wage industrial hub with modern logistics, and his personal charm which foreign investors found irresistible, Bo Xilai reportedly increased Chongqing's GDP growth from an annual average of 10.7 per cent before 2007 to a new average of 15.3 per cent, despite the Global Financial Crisis.

By 2011, Chongqing had moved from the twenty-sixth spot to the first position, and was at the very top of the pile, in terms of GDP growth in China's provinces. The city's revenues tripled and foreign direct investment in 2012 touched over US $10 billion during his time in Chongqing.[3] And that was not all. He also launched a massive social housing campaign, improved the quality of city life and tackled urban crime by smashing the mafia. All his actions had a strongly populist flavour. It harked back to the nostalgia of Maoist China where people were safer and more equal and when life was much simpler. It was called the 'Chongqing model', and it came to the attention of the central leadership in Beijing just around the time that Bo decided he had to climb the highest rung of power – the Politburo Standing Committee of the Party. There were reports that Bo Xilai was already being considered for promotion at the approaching Party's congress in 2012, but he was not the sort of person to leave anything to chance. He systematically began to build his image as a populist by tapping into the pro-Mao nostalgia. He cultivated powerful constituencies like the PLA in his area. He organized events in Chongqing for the Party's ninetieth anniversary that publicly advertised his achievements.[4] *Time* magazine named him as one among the 'World's 100 Most Influential People' of 2010.[5]

Then, all of a sudden, it all fell apart. A British businessman, Neil Heywood, was found dead, apparently poisoned, in the Lucky Holiday Hotel in Chongqing on 15 November 2011. If official Chinese reports are to be believed, the murder had been committed by Bo Xilai's wife, Gu Kailai,[6] and covered up by Police Chief Wang Lijun allegedly on Bo Xilai's orders. The subsequent falling out between Bo and his police chief had led to Wang's flight to the American consulate and his subsequent arrest. Bo's unsuccessful attempts to quash the investigation with the help of powerful people in Beijing, and his outreach to the PLA and the internal security establishment (through his alleged ally Zhou Yongkang, who was the security czar in the Politburo Standing Committee of the Party) to hold on to his power, were evidently threatening enough to cause deep alarm in the highest echelons of the Party. It spelt his end. The leadership feared that an alternate power centre was being formed, which would likely split the Party's unity and cohesion, something that the Party and its leadership had zealously worked at maintaining after the 1989 Tiananmen Incident. They decided that it was in the Party's best interests, as well as their own, that Bo Xilai was neutralized.[7] He was summarily dismissed from his official and Party positions in 2012 and, in a show trial at the end of that year he was sentenced to life imprisonment in Qincheng prison in Beijing. (His wife Gu Kailai was given a suspended death sentence for the murder of Heywood, which was subsequently commuted to life imprisonment.) The sordid details of his gross corruption and misuse of office for personal enrichment were placed on public display.

The Bo Xilai affair reverberated through the entire political system in China and starkly exposed the Party's dark side to the public on multiple fronts. First, it revealed the brittleness of China's political system. Despite the two decades of 'collective responsibility' and faceless leadership (as compared with Mao's cult of personality) since 1989, which Deng had instituted because it would prevent infighting and keep political stability, the scandal showed that ambitious individuals with power and credentials could still buck the system and shake the Party's unity in the absence of a veteran leader with unquestioned authority. Second, it exposed the deep rifts and factional rivalries inside the Party. In the month after Wang Lijun's arrest, Bo Xilai is believed to have manipulated senior figures inside the security and propaganda apparatus, and the PLA, to help him out of his predicament.[8] Third, and most tellingly for the Chinese people, it shone a light on the sordid nexus between the Chinese Communist Party, big businesses and corruption in very high places. Although prominent political figures like Chen Xitong (Beijing's party secretary) and Chen Liangyu (Shanghai's party secretary) had been pulled down on charges of gross corruption in 1996 and 2006, respectively, in this specific instance, the deadly mix of politics, money and the public support for Bo Xilai because of his 'red prince' appeal fired the public imagination. The revelations about Bo's corruption and the deep connections between him and big business hinted at an even uglier truth – in the short space of twenty years, a party that had championed the working classes of China had degenerated into one that thrived on state capitalism, and built a cosy yet profitable nexus between leaders and their business cronies.

Ironically, it was the economic reforms that Deng had begun, and which his two successors had built upon, that were, in large part, responsible for this situation. In the two decades after the Tiananmen Incident, China fundamentally transformed itself and drew the world's attention and admiration. Beneath the surface, however, and far from the public gaze, at least in the initial period, the economic forces that the reform-and-opening up policies had unleashed were also transforming the very nature of the Chinese Communist Party. Deng's southern tour in 1992 had resolved the basic political question over the direction of economic reforms. With the fading away of economic conservatives like Chen Yun and Li Xiannian in the mid-1990s, the 'leftists' within the Party had also been greatly weakened, though not entirely eliminated. In 1993, Deng's successor, General Secretary (and President) Jiang Zemin coined a new term to characterize the new policy direction set by Deng. Henceforth, China would strive to establish a 'socialist market economy'. This nomenclature, prima facie, suggested that China was still socialist. In reality, it fundamentally redefined the state's role in the economy.[9] From this point on, China moved in the direction of state capitalism. The year 1993 thus marked a decisive turning away from Mao's vision for communist China. It completed the ideological liberation of China from Maoist economics.

The Party brought fresh faces to Beijing to implement the new policy that would liberate economic forces from the straitjacket of socialism. Zhu Rongji, the party secretary of Shanghai, who was known for his no-nonsense approach and fiery temper, was chosen to steer the new course. After Zhu became the premier of the State Council in 1998, he started his term by completing the agricultural reforms that Deng had begun in 1980, by establishing a nationwide grain market that would boost rural growth and increase rural consumption. He had used the Asian financial crisis to tackle financial and tax reforms. He had reduced the size of the Chinese bureaucracy and controlled petty corruption while improving delivery. And he had reformed the cradle-to-grave welfare system that Mao and Zhou had crafted. The left-wing of the Party, which had maintained balance in the 1980s, ensuring that things did not tilt too far in the direction of capitalism, saw the dismantling of the welfare state system by Jiang and Zhu as an ideological betrayal of communist doctrine, and portrayed it as an abandonment of the workers and peasants on whose backs the Party had ridden to power. In 1995, the arch-ideologue, Deng Liqun, and what remained of the 'left', launched a series of critiques about the reforms – known as the '10,000-character manifestos'. They claimed that China was losing its independence and sovereignty to the West by taking the capitalist path.[10] Comparisons were drawn between Zhu and Gorbachev – the Soviet leader whom the Chinese hard-liners blamed for the collapse of Soviet communism. Jiang Zemin and Zhu Rongji had, however, read the public mood correctly. The Chinese people were exhausted from years of mass political campaigns and propaganda and were more interested in how they might improve their livelihood than in politics. The leftists inside the Party were quickly neutralized and Zhu carried on with reforms. In his farewell speech to the State Council in January 2003, Zhu remarked that if these hard steps had not been taken to improve and refine the social welfare system, 'we would not have today's optimistic environment'.[11] The two reforms that had the greatest bearing on the trajectory of the Chinese Communist Party in the 1990s were the restructuring of the state-owned enterprises (SOEs) and the monetization of land. Both unleashed the tsunami that would modernize China and make it the world's economic powerhouse, but they also unleashed powerful new forces that would fundamentally change the Party. A more detailed understanding of how this happened is, therefore, warranted.

The SOEs (similar to India's public sector undertakings) had been the pride and joy of Maoist China. Mao believed that they could in time rival the largest corporations of the West and lead China into the industrial and modern era. By 1994, however, 50 per cent of them were loss-making and nearly 80 per cent of their earnings were dedicated to debt servicing.[12] The Party decided to reform the public sector by consolidating the large SOEs under state control while divesting the rest into non-governmental hands (this policy was known as *zhuangda fangxiao*). As a result of the divestment of smaller SOEs, from 2000 to 2009, according to one study, the number of registered private companies in China grew by 30 per cent. Within a decade of bringing in the policy, that is by the year 2010, nearly 70 per cent of the GDP apparently came from non-state-owned enterprises.[13] The second major reform – the monetization of land – would have even greater implications for the growth of China's economy. Constitutionally and legally, all land in China belonged to the state and could not be owned privately. In the post-Tiananmen period, when the flow of foreign capital was briefly interrupted, the leadership decided to monetize the land by selling time-limited rights (lease).

Parcels of land in prime areas in major Chinese urban centres were offered to developers in return for money, which allowed the government to advance infrastructure projects that private developers were reluctant to finance. As a result of this, from 2002 until 2012, China witnessed a building boom that fundamentally transformed its urban landscape. While the private developers built the vast commercial and residential complexes that dot the Chinese urban landscape today, the central and provincial governments used the money from land-lease sales to create dazzling infrastructure. Small provincial towns got highways, airports and metros. Ports were modernized and power stations were built to address critical supply-side shortages. China began to build over 20,000 kilometres of high-speed rail. This modernization of infrastructure came just in time for China to draw the full benefits from the post-Cold War trends of globalization and international supply chains. China chalked up spectacular double-digit annual GDP growth for twenty straight years and became the world's factory. In hindsight, there is no doubt that the reforms, especially the divestment of SOEs and the monetization of land, in the Jiang–Hu era were the bedrock for China's spectacular economic growth and the resulting prosperity.

Less evident at the beginning were the inherent dangers that these policies and developments posed to the Chinese Communist Party. However, it gradually became clear that the Party's post-1993 economic policies also had a dark underside. The divestment of SOEs and the monetization of land led to corruption on an unprecedented scale in China. A significant number of divested SOEs were acquired by individuals who were related to members of the Party, or were their cronies. The divested assets were bought cheaply because officials had deliberately undervalued many of them before the sale, and then assisted their relatives and cronies to acquire them by borrowing money from state-owned banks to finance the turnaround. Party officials thus indirectly enriched themselves by benefitting their own families and friends.[14] One estimate puts the losses due to the sell-off of state assets during this period at US $41 billion.[15] Although the economy had boomed as a result of the privatization of SOEs after 1998, a significant portion of new wealth was disproportionately held by Party members themselves or their cronies, and had not percolated down to the wider society. Given the power that local governments across China had in making such divestment decisions, including whom they could sell to, it is not surprising that corruption also entered the administrative system through the sale of government offices. Graft, therefore, boomed along with the economy.

The larger SOEs had remained under the Party's control. Here, the top management positions were reserved exclusively for Party members. Although these SOEs were nominally under the state's control, it was the Party's Central Organization Department –responsible for overseeing all cadre promotions and transfers – that made all the senior appointments. A significant proportion of them were influential Party members who were on their way up the political ladder. In 2003, President Hu Jintao tightened the Party's grip on the large SOEs when he created the State-owned Assets Supervision and Administration Commission (SASAC) to centralize control over them. The idea was to create monopolies or quasi-monopolies that, along with the control that the Party exercised through its nominees on the boards, soon formed the core of the Party's patronage and power after 2003. It grew wealthy from the steady flow of cash. It is widely reported that many of these SOEs faked invoices to overbill the state and diverted contracts and customers to companies run by families and cronies of senior leaders. One China scholar used the phrase 'the mama is poor but her kids are rich' to describe the scale at which SOEs were being milked by the Party and its high-ranking members to enrich themselves.[16]

If the SOEs were important cash cows for the Party, they were rapidly dwarfed by the cash that flowed in to the Party through the monetization of land. Local governments and provincial leaders who had the authority to decide which land rights to lease, and to whom, were offered huge kickbacks in the form of property and money by private developers. Prime lots in urban centres were identified and farmed out to developers unmindful of the communities that had lived there for generations. In many cases, this led to the wholesale destruction of old cities and towns across China. Families were evicted and entire neighbourhoods were razed, including those that contained heritage buildings and culturally significant places. A large part of central Beijing near the Tiananmen Square, which was dotted with courtyard homes (*siheyuan*) of the erstwhile Manchu nobility, vanished. Nanjing's mayor, Ji Jianye, who was later convicted for gross corruption, is believed to have ordered the demolition of over ten million square metres of buildings within a single year, which was routed to developers and cronies for profit.[17] New cities mushroomed. City centres across China were entirely transformed into glass and concrete towers. A real estate boom ensued as millions of Chinese rushed to buy homes. So much construction activity was taking place that, within the diplomatic corps and expatriate community, the joke was that the crane had become China's national bird. It was rumoured that China consumed more steel, cement and glass within the first decade of the twenty-first century than the United States of America had consumed in the entire course of the twentieth century. Along with the high rises that rose in China's cities, rose the mountain of corruption. Corruption soon reached unprecedented levels and became deeply entrenched, indeed institutionalized, within the Party. It became a pyramid of money and power. At the top of this money pile sat the 'princelings' (*tai zi*).

The princelings were the children and descendants of the first generation of communist revolutionaries who had maintained their influence in the system through personal connections (known colloquially as *guan xi*). At the apex of this elite group were the so-called imperial families, including the descendants of the 'eight immortals' who claimed their inheritance on the basis of bloodline.[18] In the past, the patriarchs of such families had lived and worked together in Zhongnanhai (part of the imperial palace that Mao had reserved for the top cadres after 1949), and their descendants shared close social bonds that were leveraged in the 1980s for advancement. Part of the political bargain that Deng had struck with the other ageing leaders, in order to persuade them to relinquish their political power, was to permit one family member to preserve their interests. A newly entitled red aristocracy was born just as China was opening up to the outside world. They were ideally placed to benefit from the first wave of SOE divestment and monetization of land. None of them had inherited personal wealth but they had inherited influence that could provide others with access to the leadership – an impossible prospect for ordinary Chinese – and they could influence policy in favour of the new entrepreneurial class that was emerging as a result of the reforms.

Over time these 'imperial families' began to dominate key economic sectors – Jiang Zemin's family was into telecommunications, Li Peng's family was in energy, Deng Xiaoping's children had deep roots in the property sector, Wang Zhen's son headed a major arms manufacturer (Poly Group) and Chen Yun's son headed the China Development Bank. Others headed SOE conglomerates, giving them access to wealth through contracts and deals. Still others entered politics – Bo Xilai, Ye Xuanping (son of Marshal Ye Jiangying) and Xi Jinping among them – and facilitated their family businesses. One of the most egregious examples of this was Premier Wen Jiabao. Wen did not, ostensibly, have any property or wealth (his salary was reported to be only US $15,000 per month). But in October 2012, the *New York Times* published an exposé on his family's wealth, including that of his spouse who was neck-deep into the market for diamonds. (By 2010, China had become among the world's largest consumers of diamond jewellery.) His daughter, Wen Ruchun, had set up a consulting company (Fullmark) with just two employees and was reportedly being paid close to one million dollars in fees to 'facilitate' a deal for the American bank JP Morgan Chase with the state-run China Railway group for an IPO worth US $5 billion.[19] In 2012, Bloomberg's analysis of the wealth of the descendants of the 'eight immortals' network claimed that of the 103 descendants that they had tracked, 43 headed their own companies and a further 26 held top jobs in SOEs.[20] Corruption at the top was common knowledge. In 1996, Zhu Rongji famously said, 'To fight corruption one must go after the tiger first, then the wolf. There will be absolutely no tolerance for the tiger.'[21] Occasionally a big 'tiger' (as well-connected and highly placed party cadres were known) fell to corruption, like Shanghai's party secretary Chen Liangyu or Nanjing's mayor Ji Jianye. But these were exceptions, the result of political vendettas. In the main, the

Party grew progressively corrupt and the families of the top leaders amassed massive fortunes.

Below these princelings and descendants of high-ranking central cadres were the provincial and local officials who enjoyed substantial powers to take economic decisions affecting their communities. Yuen Yuen Ang's book, *China's Gilded Age*, shows how businesspersons gained government favours in exchange for 'access money' – the term used for the payment of bribes by businesspersons to CCP officials in return for facilitating contacts with the senior decision-makers. The provincial or local officials benefitted in two ways. At the personal level, they collected money or leveraged their power in order to secure business, employment or properties for their family members. At the official level, they came to the notice of the higher-ups for delivering economic output. In the 1990s and 2000s, the leadership judged the performance of cadres in numbers – that is, GDP growth. The more the local economy prospered, the more likely it was that their economic performance would impress their superiors in the Party, and the more likely they were to get on to the path to higher office and also, potentially, to more money in the future. It became a virtuous cycle. Yuen Yuen Ang called it a profit-sharing model between the Party-state and the cadre-official, both of whom developed official and personal stakes in the booming Chinese economy.[22] Richard Smith called this phenomenon the 'marketization of power'.[23]

Even further down in the pecking order was the bureaucrat whose formal salary was very low. The Party saw to it that they too got a personal stake in the profits, in return for delivering government services efficiently. Prequisites included foreign travel and training abroad, free and expensive meals, vacations, subsidized housing in choice parts of the town and access to entertainment. This marketization of power was not limited to the civilian bureaucracy. The security forces – the People's Liberation Army, the People's Armed Police (PAP), and the Public Security Bureau (PSB) – also climbed on to the bandwagon. By the late 1990s, the PLA, PAP and PSB were managing a wide range of businesses, from tourism and entertainment services to the sale of Chinese weaponry to foreign governments. The efforts by Jiang Zemin and Hu Jintao to curb the security services' penchant for doing business in exchange for substantially enhanced budgetary incentives were never able to completely eliminate the phenomenon. Throughout the twenty years between 1992 and 2012, the PLA and PAP continued to profit institutionally and personally from their vast business enterprises.

The sheer volumes of money that were being generated through grand corruption manifested in the sales of high-end luxury goods. China quickly became the world's third-largest market for fine French wines and cognac, expensive watches, ladies' handbags and top-end vehicles. According to a report by Ernst & Young, in 2005 China accounted for 12 per cent of global sales of luxury products and generated more than US $2 billion in sales a year, which was projected to exceed US $11.5 billion by 2010.[24] It was difficult to reconcile this obvious wealth on display in Beijing and Shanghai with the fact that in China the average annual per capita income was less than US $1,200 at that time. Apparently, few people cared about the reality and most grew quickly impressed by the dazzling displays of wealth by an infinitesimal number of Party members and their business cronies. Western manufacturers of luxury products salivated at the profit margins because those with money in China were ready to pay many times the price for luxury goods, as a means of making a social statement or as a demonstration of their power and status in the new China. These were the years of global admiration for the Chinese Communist

Party's governance model and its apparent capacity to create growth in comparison with the rest of the world. High levels of corruption were justified by the argument that not all types of corruption necessarily hurt growth. Foreigners sometimes even chose to extol the efficiencies of 'managed politics', which was a palatable way of describing the process of unilateral decision-making by an authoritarian regime.

The entry of big money brought changes to the Party's membership. A new class of people had emerged in Chinese society. It was variously labelled as the entrepreneurial class or the middle class. Urbanization, rapid industrialization and China's entry into the WTO had all catalysed the emergence of this class quicker than in other similarly placed economies. They were the beneficiaries of China's modernization and reform, mostly urban and well-educated, but they had no stakes in China's political system. Up to that point, the Communist Party of China had continued to call itself the bastion of workers and peasants. The Tiananmen Incident had begun to make the Party aware of how the opening up of China to the outside world might have impacted Chinese society and thinking. The Party grew concerned that this educated and increasingly prosperous class of people, who were outside the pale of politics, might turn towards other ideas, like democracy and rule of law. It was Jiang Zemin's idea to co-opt them into the Party as a means of neutralizing a potential problem. Yet, that was easier said than done. He had to take several steps to create the environment and prepare the Party for the shift. He began this process by declaring that the Party had the ability to accommodate those who were not workers and peasants. He prepared the ground with a speech just before the Fifteenth Party Congress, saying 'any form of ownership that meets the criteria of the Three Represents can and should be utilized to serve socialism'.[25,26] The next step was to legitimize the role of private enterprise in the Party's eyes and statutes. In 1999, he got the Party to acknowledge the role of private enterprise in the constitution as an important component of the socialist market economy. After doing that, in July 2001, Jiang Zemin gave a speech on the eightieth anniversary of the Party's founding, proposing criteria to co-opt the new category of members, thus finally opening the door for them to become bona fide members, provided that they toed the Party line. This new constituency included not only entrepreneurs, but also intellectuals, university graduates, and the urban middle class in coastal China. According to one estimate, students and entrepreneurs soon became the fastest-growing sources of new members for the Party, increasing at the rate of 255 per cent and 113 per cent, respectively, between 2002 and 2007.[27] Students discovered that embracing the Party gave them access to networks that were crucial in furthering their professional careers. Intellectuals and academics, who had in the past faced criticism, boycott and even violence for their views during the ideological shifts in the Maoist years, saw membership as an inside track to ensuring that they got an early indication of which way the wind was blowing, politically speaking, as well as a means for intellectual advancement. Business persons sought membership for access as well as for protection from the caprice of officials, and also because it conferred social respectability.[28] By the time Hu Jintao succeeded Jiang Zemin as the president in March 2003, what was once a revolutionary party had been transformed into an urban party of business.

Membership was not the only way in which the Party changed in these years. Money also had an impact on its internal dynamics. With the passing of the old guard, many of the old networks based on pre-revolutionary ties all but vanished. Deng's insistence on the primacy of collective leadership, the overriding importance of maintaining political stability and adhering to the consensus on economic reforms also ensured that the policy fights, which had roiled the party in the 1980s, gradually diminished. The internal fights were now increasingly about power and money.[29] The money trail began at the top of the Party. Those lower down soon realized that their promotion and financial well-being were linked to members who were higher up in the chain, and began to align themselves accordingly. Inevitably, factionalism, which Deng had warned the Party against, reared its head again. Only this time, unlike in the eras of Mao and Deng, it was not based on personal connections (*guan xi*) alone, nor social intimacy or ideological orientation, but instead on money. The most prominent of the factions was the 'Shanghai gang', led by Jiang Zemin and his associates, including Huang Ju, Wu Bangguo and the éminence grise of Jiang's China, Zeng Qinghong. Then there was the Communist Youth League faction – known in China as the *tuan pai* and considered a staging-ground for future leaders – headed by Hu Jintao. This group included Li Keqiang, who is currently the premier of the State Council. A technocratic faction, loosely known as the 'Qinghua faction', because its members had studied at the prestigious Qinghua University, provided many of the politburo and cabinet members under Presidents Jiang and Hu. Premier Wen Jiabao was one such member. The Li Peng faction, although a declining force by the end of the century, was still influential in some matters due to the influence that Li Peng wielded among the conservative members of the Party. By and large, factional rivalries were managed within the rules of collective responsibility that Deng had imposed on the Party after 1989, but there were instances when the conjunction of power and money led to purges within the leadership. Such purges were intended to send a political message about who was ruling the roost. Thus, the removal and imprisonment of Chen Liangyu, party secretary of Shanghai, during the era of President Hu Jintao, was a message to the Shanghai gang as to who held the reins of power. As a result of the growth of factionalism inside the Party, the centralization of power in the hands of a dominant leader virtually disappeared after Deng's death in 1997. Power became dispersed among the several members of the Politburo Standing Committee and a few retired Party veterans.

One point that all factions could agree upon was that the PLA should not be allowed to form a faction or to play any direct political role, and should be subordinated to the Party's absolute control. Mao Zedong had kept the PLA on a tight leash, but during the Cultural Revolution he needed them to neutralize his opponents and later to manage the Red Guards who were out of control by 1968. As a result, the PLA had reacquired political power and, due to their pre-revolutionary ties with the Old Guard, were able to retain it even after the Cultural Revolution had ended in 1976. Deng's deep pre-revolutionary ties to the military had ensured that the PLA remained subordinate to the Party, but the 1989 incident had also shown how its absolute leadership over the PLA had dangerously weakened. (According to reports, General Xu Qinxian, commander of the 38th Army, who was charged with clearing the Square, had balked at the orders and was court-martialled after 4 June.) Concerns about the PLA's loyalty to the Party were exacerbated after the Communist Party of the Soviet Union collapsed in 1991. The Party's assessment was that the Soviet Red Army had failed to come to the rescue of the CPSU. Deng and other leaders became more aware that

General Yang Shangkun, president of China at the time of the Tiananmen Incident, and his half-brother General Yang Baibing, who headed the PLA's General Political Department and was, therefore, the chief political commissar, were building influence within the PLA after 1989. The leadership might have suspected that a military faction was in the making. Although the brothers had publicly backed Deng on his economic reforms during his southern tour in 1992, the Party quickly relieved Yang Baibing from his post later that year. After Yang Shangkun had stepped down as China's president in 1993, Deng also oversaw the transfer of authority over the Central Military Commission to the new general secretary, Jiang Zemin, in the belief that personal control by Party leaders over the PLA was coming to an end with the passing of the generation of revolutionaries, and there was an urgent need to institutionalize the authority over the PLA in the person of the general secretary of the Chinese Communist Party.[30] This was in the common interest of all factions in the Party. By 1997, the last military representative (Admiral Liu Huaqing) in the Party's apex organ – the Politburo Standing Committee (PBSC) – was eased out. No PLA representative has ever again been appointed to the PBSC thereafter.

Although Jiang Zemin smoothly assumed control over the military from Deng, the PLA continued to remain influential in Chinese politics because of its historical role and because the Party considered the PLA to be its sword-arm. Jiang, therefore, had to evolve a new style of civil–military relationship since, unlike Mao and Deng, he had not served alongside the PLA. He, therefore, created a new deal. In return for the PLA's assurances that it would support the Party's policy of reform and opening up and that it would act as the guarantor of the Party's absolute rule, the Party agreed to respect the military's professional independence and to support its modernization. In practice, this meant that the Party took good care of the PLA's interests and, in return, there was no overt military participation in the factional struggles as the civilian leaders jockeyed for money and power. This distinctly new arrangement that evolved between the general secretary and the PLA in the post-Deng period permitted Jiang Zemin and his successor Hu Jintao to stay at the helm as chairmen of the Central Military Commission, as per the arrangement laid down by Deng, but neither of them interfered in day-to-day military matters. One expert commentator described the new arrangement as 'reigning but not ruling'.[31] Although this arrangement worked reasonably well for twenty years, there were long-term implications for the Party that were not so good. It encouraged fragmentation of the Party's authority and introduced new challenges to ensuring the PLA's loyalty. The generals had been given a free hand in promotions, and the sale of military offices had become a common practice by the end of Hu Jintao's second term. Generals Guo Boxiong and Xu Caihou, who served as vice-chairmen of the Central Military Commission under Hu Jintao, allegedly sold military offices for vast profits and had made great sums of money through PLA purchasing contracts and arms sales. (Both were eventually convicted of gross corruption by Xi Jinping with the objective of re-asserting control over the military after 2013.) By the end of Hu Jintao's presidency in 2013, both the PLA and their cousins, the People's Armed Police (PAP) and the Public Security Bureau (PSB) were akin to quasi-independent power centres. (The PAP and PSB had come under the control of Zhou Yongkang, China's security czar on the Politburo Standing Committee. His role in the Bo Xilai affair and the accumulation of power made him the first major target for Xi Jinping's purges.)

The most significant change that took place in the Chinese Communist Party during the Jiang–Hu period was, however, the disappearance of ideology. Deng had closed the door on the extreme ideology that Mao had practised during the Cultural Revolution, and had substituted it with a new lexicon of Chinese communism that included phrases such as 'socialism with Chinese characteristics' and 'socialist market economy', to support the Party's new economic line. Jiang and Hu continued with this approach. As the economy developed and China opened up to the outside world, classical communist ideology looked more and more archaic. In June 1949, on the eve of the revolution, Mao had once declared that the people's democratic dictatorship would be based 'mainly on the alliance of the workers and the peasants'. He had also said that the 'monopoly capitalist class will be eliminated for good', and that the arrival of socialism in China would mean the 'nationalization of private enterprise'. Mao had called the United States and its allies 'imperialists and their running dogs' and rejected the notion that their assistance was needed by China for its development.[32] Yet, by the end of the 1990s, the bourgeois classes were being readmitted into the Party, nationalized enterprises were being handed back to private entrepreneurs and the countries of the West had become some of China's most favoured partners in economic development. The fading away of classical Maoism was thus, in some sense, a natural consequence of the economic reform and the dismantling of the cradle-to-grave welfare system (iron rice bowl). Inside the Party, the ideological campaigns and pre-revolutionary networks that had held it together were being replaced by new ties based on money and power. But the Party still needed a new narrative in order to retain political legitimacy in the eyes of the Chinese people. The urban–rural divide, the growing income disparities, the dissolution of the welfare system, the reform of the SOEs, which led to worker layoffs, and the displacement of people from their homes were all contributing to public unhappiness.

Officially, 'socialism with Chinese characteristics' remained the main ideological line for the Party, but nationalism began to emerge as an attractive alternative. After Tiananmen, the Party started a mass 'patriotic education' campaign to re-invent itself in the eyes of the Chinese people. China was rising and the Party positioned itself as the vanguard of national rejuvenation. It played up China's historic role as a glorious civilization (*wenming guguo*) and global economic power before circa 1850 and played down the domestic weaknesses that had caused China's decline after the mid-nineteenth century. Instead, the Party vociferously proclaimed that China had fallen from its high perch after 1840 because it had been a victim of bullying by outside powers. The Party called it China's 'century of humiliation' by the West and Japan, defined as the period from the start of the Anglo-Chinese (Opium) war of 1840 to the 'liberation of China' by the Chinese Communist Party in 1949. The victimization narrative was embedded deeply through the patriotic education campaign and inserted into Party documents and in official media, as well as in school and university textbooks. A whole generation of Chinese after 1989 thus came of age believing that all the trouble that China had faced in the last century and a half, beginning with the perceived loss of territory during the colonial period, was the fault of the foreigner. The Party also cleverly claimed the entire credit for rescuing China from this humiliating situation in 1949 – Chiang Kai-shek and his nationalist government had been airbrushed out of the picture, although they had borne the brunt of the fighting after the Japanese invasion. The Chinese people were told that it was only the Communist Party of China that would be able to restore their national honour and dignity and guarantee China's proper place at the top of the global order. In 1996, Jiang Zemin proclaimed 'the Chinese Communist Party is the firmest, the most thoroughgoing patriot', wrapping the Party in the national flag so that support for it became the highest act of patriotism for the people.[33] Those who disputed this narrative became, by extension, unpatriotic. This new ultra-nationalistic path that the Party adopted after 1989 also fused it and the state into a single inseparable entity, making the security of one the security of the other.

Other governments have, from time to time, wrapped themselves similarly in the national flag. In this case, there was an important difference. The Chinese Communist Party practised an aggressive form of nationalism. It manipulated public opinion by identifying specific enemies and channelling mass anger against them. It created new bogies like the 'China threat' or the 'containment' theory. It claimed that the foreigners were jealous of China's rise. Legitimate unhappiness over Chinese behaviour, such as anti-dumping activities against undervalued Chinese goods, or international criticism about its aggressive actions in the South China Sea or on the borders with India, were explained away as unfair and discriminatory. The mistakes that the Party had made in the half century of its rule, some of which, like the Great Leap Forward or the Great Proletarian Cultural Revolution, had resulted in the death by starvation or incarceration of millions of Chinese people, were blurred and no responsibility was fixed on the leaders who had allowed this to happen. It was as if the Chinese Communist Party had done no wrong to the Chinese people. On the contrary, the leaders had rescued the Chinese people by holding high the flag of national pride and rejuvenation. In the Jiang–Hu period, many outsiders believed, erroneously as it turned out, that the particular brand of nationalism adopted by the Party was a temporary natural reaction to the shame and humiliation that China felt as a result of its treatment by the West during the so-called century of humiliation.[34] Such thinking failed to take into account the political motivation for such a narrative. Despite its apparent power and strength, the Chinese Communist Party was paranoid about its legitimacy and security. It used patriotism (*aiguo zhuyi*) as the tool to bind the people to its cause.

How could the world's largest communist party mask this reality from the rest of the world during the Jiang–Hu era? Perception management played a big part. The personality cult, the mass campaigns and the polemics of Maoist China – they described the Americans as capitalist roaders, the Europeans as running dogs of imperialism, the Soviets as revisionists, the Indians as lackeys of the West, and so on – were replaced by benign images of staid and sober leaders devoid of charisma and demagoguery, who practised collective responsibility and handed over power in an orderly fashion as a result of age and term limits.[35] Every five years, from 1993 to 2013, the Chinese leaders with brushed-back, jet-black hair and wearing dark, Western-style suits and matching ties would walk out onto the stage in protocol order to introduce themselves to the international media. The world would be reassured that the Communist Party of China had changed and was becoming more like a normal political party. Foreign media would extol the many excellent qualities of the new leaders on the basis of information fed to them by 'sources'. The communist leaders cleverly appropriated and used concepts which lay at the heart of Western civilization – democracy, constitution, rule of law and human rights – to soothe and lull the rest of the world into believing that they were open, transparent, democratic and believed in a universal set of values. In March each year, when the rubber-stamp bicameral legislature – National People's Congress and the Chinese People's Political Consultative Committee – held their annual two-week show in Beijing, the extensive media coverage was used to show how China was steadily moving towards the rule of law. The premier of the State Council would submit his annual work report to the National People's Congress in the presence of the foreign diplomatic corps and the media, just like the president of the United States would outline his vision in the State of the Union Address. Certain sessions were thrown open for public viewing and foreign diplomats were invited to witness the vote on important pieces of legislation. And the foreign press was always briefed on how the president of China and other holders of public office were elected, including the number of nay-votes that they received, in order to demonstrate that free will existed in Chinese politics. In reality, there was no separation of powers because this was not within the scope of a single-party state. Legislators were not directly elected by universal suffrage. Nor were legislative debates, if they actually took place, televised or open to public viewing, as is the case in normal democratic parliaments. The annual meeting of the two bodies (*liang hui*) was pure theatre for the Chinese people and the outside world. When such obvious shortcomings were pointed out by a few, the Chinese would quickly claim what they were practising was a form of democracy with 'Chinese characteristics'. The world pretended for twenty-five years after 1989 that this would eventually evolve into some reflection of Western-style governance, rarely willing to admit that, for all its talk of political reform, the Party maintained a choke-hold on the state throughout this period.[36]

There was ample evidence about how the Party actually functioned after Tiananmen. It was common knowledge, for instance, that before any major event, security arrangements in Beijing were greatly enhanced, internet cafes and other regular meeting-spots for foreigners with Chinese people were closely watched, outsiders who might cause any kind of trouble were debarred from entering the capital, activists were placed under temporary house arrest and even Tiananmen Square was barricaded off so that ordinary citizens could not stage flash protests. Tibet and other minority areas were closed off to foreigners, and Tibetans, in particular, were looked upon with deep distrust by security authorities in China. The foreign press and diplomatic corps were aware that for all the Party's talk about freedom and democracy, nascent political movements like the China Democracy Forum or spiritual movements like Fa Lun Gong were suppressed and outlawed. Yet, this was rarely written about in those years. The mainstream media as well as diplomatic missions in Beijing either fell for the 'makeover' or chose to ignore inconvenient facts.

This Chinese makeover extended beyond politics to the world of business and industry. In order to attract vast sums of foreign direct investment, especially into the larger SOEs that were controlled by the Party, it consciously had to show that it was taking a back seat so that its heavy hand was not visible to the outside world. The reality of the Party's supervision over the SOEs was replaced by the myth that these were commercial entities that, like Western business conglomerates and trans-national corporations, were driven by profit. Western and Japanese trans-national corporations rushed into joint ventures and technology-sharing agreements. So much foreign money flowed into the country after that that as one China expert put it, 'if in the 1990s, Beijing had been worried about keeping the companies (SOEs) afloat, early in the new century the restructured companies were so big and ambitious that the problem was of how to keep them in line.'[37] The fact that these companies were under the Party's control, as well as being instruments of national policy, was rarely spoken about in the foreign business community. Even when it became more overtly interventionist in the mid-2000s, by re-energizing party cells in Sino–foreign joint ventures, and started to promote mergers and acquisitions between Chinese SOEs in order to create monopolies that benefitted the Chinese and disadvantaged the competition, or when SOEs began to target foreign companies with cutting-edge technologies in areas of business that had been of marginal interest to them till then.

A new generation of Chinese intellectuals and academics, who were newly minted members of the Party, were drafted to engage the West and provide the intellectual justification for China's rise and to craft the image of China's integration into the global order. The Party encouraged them to build strong ties to Western universities, think tanks and research institutions. This was the era of major tie-ups between Chinese and foreign universities. Foreign universities and think tanks set up branches inside prominent Chinese universities. In turn, China established Confucius Institutes worldwide. Tens of thousands of Chinese students, many with significant state funding, flooded American educational and research institutions, professing their desire to learn all about America. They were given exceptional access to universities and laboratories, all of which were eager for a share of China's education pie. People knew that the Party maintained tight control over the activities of Chinese students, scientists and intellectuals abroad, that it monitored their writings and controlled what they published, but the signs were ignored. All doors were opened for the Chinese.

Domestically, the Party demonstrated great skill in maintaining tight social control while dumping the authoritarian straitjacket.[38]

It consciously retreated from the private lives of individuals and citizens. This had a liberating effect on society as a whole. Entrepreneurship and business flourished under the Party's protection. Academic institutions and intellectuals were permitted foreign contact and travel as long as they did not stray from the Party's narrative. The student community was encouraged to study abroad and assured of successful careers in business and politics. The world of culture was permitted to step away from ideologically inspired or motivated work. They were free to explore, albeit within clearly defined boundaries. There was an explosion of cultural experimentation and output during this period. Science and research also vastly benefitted from the active encouragement that the Party gave to its scientists to travel abroad, do joint experimentation with Western countries and establish laboratories in key Chinese institutions with foreign assistance and technical support. There was one basic condition that all of Chinese society had to follow. No politics. So long as there was no criticism of the Party and its leaders, or any efforts to build alternative narratives and organizations, the Jiang–Hu era was one in which individual Chinese could grow and prosper in ways that they were unable to do earlier.

Overall, after Tiananmen, the Communist Party of China displayed adaptability to change and the capacity to deal with an uncertain international environment. Unlike its Soviet counterpart, it was not ideologically hidebound, nor incapacitated by gerontocratic leadership. The Party was pragmatic, its leaders were educated and technically qualified for the post-Cold War digital age, and its policies were adapted to the people's needs. It did whatever was necessary to keep its legitimacy in the eyes of the people. There were challenges, missteps and even backtracking. The idea of the 'peaceful rise of China' created an international backlash, for example, but the Party quickly mitigated the fallout of such mistakes and took corrective measures. The Communist Party of China can take a lot of the credit for the skilful manner in which it was able to hide the truth about itself for so long, through a combination of public image-making and diplomacy, survive the end of the twentieth century and emerge in the new century as an alternative to democracy.

:CHAPTER 7:

India and China: Attempts at Modus Vivendi

THE MANAGEMENT OF INDIA'S RELATIONS WITH THE PEOPLE'S REPUBLIC of China was a high and critical priority for the Indian government in the decades after 1989. Prime Minister Rajiv Gandhi's visit from 19–23 December 1988 was the first by an Indian prime minister in thirty-four years. (Nehru had visited China as prime minister in October 1954.) Rajiv Gandhi's visit, therefore, was preceded by very careful preparation as well as the crafting of a public posture by the Indian side. The government was conscious that earlier attempts to normalize the relationship after the 1962 border war had proved abortive. In May 1970, Mao Zedong approached India's *chargé d'affaires* in Beijing, Brajesh Mishra, to convey that both countries could not be quarrelling and should be friends again.[1] In February 1979, Foreign Minister Atal Bihari Vajpayee had visited China in a fresh attempt to rebuild ties, declaring that 'one would not deny that the problems between our two countries are difficult and complex. I am, however, hopeful that a beginning would be made to explore the possibilities of resolving these problems ... .'[2] In October 1984, there was a further informal outreach to the Chinese side by the Indian side through a high-level, back-channel intermediary.[3] For one reason or another, none of these earlier efforts had borne fruit. In the meantime, an uneasy state of affairs had prevailed for nearly three decades. The relationship was again put to the test in 1986–87 when the two countries potentially came close to another border conflict, after Chinese troops had occupied an Indian patrol point in the Sumdorong Chu Valley (Wangdong to the Chinese) in the state of Arunachal Pradesh, and India had moved its military forces to the heights overlooking the valley in 1986.[4]

Both sides recognized the inherent danger and each may have had good reason to take a fresh look at the state of their relationship. From India's perspective, the international environment was growing more complicated as the West aligned with China during the final decade of the Cold War. The Soviet Union, India's friend, was also attempting its rapprochement after President Mikhail Gorbachev spoke about his readiness to engage with China at a speech in Vladivostok in July 1986. China, on its part, was proceeding down the path of reform and opening up after 1980, and needed a more favourable international environment. India, under Prime Minister Rajiv Gandhi, was also experimenting with economic reform. The changed circumstances made it possible for both sides to explore the common ground between them after the end of the Cold War. As former National Security Advisor Shivshankar Menon put it, the end of the Cold War had 'made old foreign policy certainties invalid'.[5] In the cold light of the post-Cold War international order, which was dominated by America, both India and China saw their relative vulnerabilities more clearly and both were anxious to mitigate potential American arm-twisting.[6]

Former Foreign Secretary J.N. Dixit described this as a 'parallelism if not a convergence of interests' that allowed both sides to initiate positive interaction.[7] Therefore, it suited both sides to craft a new paradigm for the India–China relationship.

In early 1988, Prime Minister Rajiv Gandhi sent P.N. Haksar as his special envoy to meet with people in Beijing, in order to assess China's attitude and indications towards India. It was Haksar's assessment that would be worthwhile for Rajiv Gandhi to pay our neighbour a visit.[8] As a result of the careful preparation, a new modus vivendi emerged from Prime Minister Rajiv Gandhi's talks with Deng Xiaoping, General Secretary Zhao Ziyang and Premier Li Peng. Both agreed that this relationship would be fully normalized and would no longer be conditional upon prior settlement of the boundary question. Second, both also committed to maintaining peace and tranquillity in the border regions pending a final settlement. It was understood that there would be no attempts to change the status quo with the use of force or the threat of use of force. Third, each acknowledged the legitimate contributions of the other to the maintenance of global peace and development. This included a tacit understanding that each would accommodate the other on multilateral issues of common concern.[9] On the boundary question, that had been front and centre in the relationship for the previous four decades, a new formulation mandated both parties to 'develop their relations actively in other fields and work hard to create a favourable climate and conditions for a fair and reasonable settlement of the boundary question while seeking a mutually acceptable solution to this question'.[10] India took this to mean that the boundary question would continue to be discussed in a new Joint Working Group (JWG) led by the Indian foreign secretary and the Chinese vice minister of foreign affairs, with the objective of finding a mutually acceptable solution. On board the special aircraft that was returning him to New Delhi, Rajiv Gandhi told the accompanying media that the JWG would also focus on maintaining tranquillity in the border regions. India, it seemed, was ready to undertake a fresh effort to resolve the deadlock on the boundary question with sincerity.

An improved relationship with India suited the Chinese as well. The years from 1987 until 1992 were traumatic for China. It had begun to fundamentally reorient its foreign policy by the mid-1980s to get more space to deal with internal adjustments. China faced massive protests from 1987, and especially in 1989, and had to deal with a strong global reaction to the Tiananmen Incident of 4 June 1989 as well as with the collapse of European communism. Their India policy was based on two assessments: first, after the Cold War had ended, like China, India preferred to see a multipolar world and, hence, improved relations with India would serve China's similar interests; and second, US-led efforts to interfere in China's domestic situation after the collapse of the Soviet Union (they saw a direct US hand in the Tiananmen Square events of 1989) required them to build insurance against the pursuit of another 'containment' strategy by the Americans. Keeping the Indians on their right side would help this process. (The Chinese had taken note of the fact that India had not been critical of the CCP's action in using military force to suppress the protests and to restore order.) According to the official history that the Chinese Communist Party released in early 2021, one of the outcomes of China's review of its foreign policy in 1989 was an improved relationship with India.[11] However, Chinese writings also suggest that this improved relationship did not, from the Chinese perspective, necessarily involve any fundamental shift in China's position (or territorial claims) on the boundary question. In the Chinese system, to the contrary, there were expectations of significant concessions from the Indian side on boundary matters.[12] The new boundary formulation in the joint press statement issued at the end of Rajiv Gandhi's visit was regarded by Beijing as a public compromise that allowed for the recasting of the boundary question. Chinese demands that India 'accommodate' China's territorial asks in Arunachal Pradesh (the eastern sector of the India–China boundary) remained unchanged. The Chinese also continued to doubt India's sincerity and to suspect its intentions with respect to the handling of the Dalai Lama and the Tibetan issue, in general.*

From India's perspective, the China–Pakistan relationship remained a constraint in the overall relationship. Their nuclear and missile cooperation continued apace after Rajiv Gandhi's visit, with no indications that the Chinese would be more sensitive to India's concerns. China's support to Pakistan also seriously coloured its position on the terrorism that Pakistan was sponsoring in Jammu and Kashmir after 1989, and gave India cause to doubt Chinese sincerity on the question of India's sovereignty and territorial integrity. Despite these limitations, both evidently still felt that there were sufficient commonalities between India and China to warrant an effort at an improvement in ties. In sum, both sides felt that the changed geopolitical circumstances and their respective domestic requirements called for an adjustment in the India–China relationship, but there were, possibly, different expectations about a satisfactory outcome on the boundary question.

---

* Until 1987 the Chinese had engaged with the Dalai Lama's representatives and even allowed them to make visits to Tibet, but this had ceased after the fall of General Secretary Hu Yaobang and the subsequent tightening of Chinese control inside Tibet Autonomous Region from then onwards.

In 1992, a new government in India under Prime Minister P.V. Narasimha Rao and a revamped Chinese leadership with President Jiang Zemin started to explore various possibilities with each other, as part of a strategic adjustment of their respective foreign policies, resulting from the global realities after the end of the Cold War. Prime Minister Rao adopted a mature and pragmatic approach. The summit-level political dialogue that had broken down in 1960 was revived – Premier Li Peng visited India in December 1991, President R. Venkataraman visited China in May 1992, Prime Minister P.V. Narasimha Rao visited China in September 1993 and President Jiang Zemin visited India in November 1996. A plethora of dialogue mechanisms – among them were the security, policy planning, counterterrorism, disarmament and non-proliferation dialogues – along with a ministerial-level joint group on economic relations and trade, created the public perception that the relationship was on the mend. People-to-people relations were re-established after visa and travel restrictions were eased on both sides. Trade relations resumed. This included border trade at Shipki La on the Himachal Pradesh–Tibet Autonomous Region border.[13] Some of the earlier bilateral arrangements that had been suspended after the 1962 border conflict were restored. Consulates were re-established in Shanghai and Mumbai (they had been closed in 1962). Although trade and other aspects of the relationship did not materialize on the ground until the early years of the twenty-first century, the overall atmosphere of bilateral relations remained congenial through most of the 1990s. This process was halted when India conducted five nuclear tests in the Pokhran desert on 11 and 13 May 1998. China saw itself as the major target of India's decision to test, and there was a hiatus in the relationship for about fourteen months until some deft diplomacy by India allowed both sides to restore normalcy in the relationship.[14]

One of the positive developments after relations had been repaired was the beginning of cooperation in matters relating to shared rivers. In 2002 China agreed to restore the pre-1959 arrangement for sharing flood-season data for the Brahmaputra river (known in Tibet as the Yarlung Tsangpo) with the Indian side. India required such data for better flood prediction and protection measures downstream in Assam, and there hangs an interesting tale. Both sides agreed on restoring the pre-1959 arrangements with alacrity but differed on the charges to be paid by India to China for the use of such data. The Chinese knew well how important such flood-season data was for India and wanted to extract a heavy financial cost. Efforts to resolve the deadlock over costs at the official level proved unsuccessful. In the meantime, a natural landslip that had blocked the flow of water in the Pare Chu river, on the Tibetan side of the boundary opposite the Indian state of Himachal Pradesh, had burst in 2000, leading to a landslide lake outburst flood (LLOF) that sent a massive wall of water into the Kinnaur district downstream and causing huge destruction on the Indian side. It came without any warning from China, and it highlighted the urgency of closer cooperation in flood prediction on trans-border rivers. Indian planners realized that the consequences would be devastating if a similar incident happened in the Yarlung Tsangpo/Brahmaputra river. In this region, too, there was a geological history of sudden blockages in the river's flow just before it entered India, especially at the Great Bend around Mt Namcha Barwa in Tibet. The Indian leadership deemed this a matter of national concern and decided to elevate it to the political level. During the visit by External Affairs Minister Jaswant Singh to China in 2002, he brought up this matter with Premier Zhu Rongji, who, on the spot, directed his officials to resume the earlier arrangements, even jokingly suggesting that

China could charge India one American dollar for the data. The whole incident boded well for India–China relations.

Progress on the boundary issue, however, seemed to elude both sides. Some experts felt that the Chinese leadership might not have been in a position to make territorial concessions to India for fear of looking weak.[15] Other experts have suggested that India might have reneged from a commitment to resolving the boundary question, which was given to the Chinese side in December 1988, though there is no public record of such a commitment being given.[16] Either way, the initial expectations that a possible boundary settlement might emerge after Rajiv Gandhi's visit faded away. Perhaps, the Chinese side may have found it more convenient to take the less onerous road of ensuring that peace and tranquillity prevailed in the border areas rather than the more politically difficult path of settling the disputed land boundary. This consideration brought the two countries to a discussion on the Line of Actual Control (LAC).

The idea of the LAC itself was a Chinese creation. Having usurped Indian territory in Aksai Chin in the 1950s, Premier Zhou Enlai claimed, in his letter of 7 November 1959 to Prime Minister Nehru, that such a line had existed between the two militaries.[17] After the border conflict in October 1962, China went on to proclaim that it had unilaterally withdrawn its military forces twenty kilometres behind this imaginary Chinese LAC as a goodwill measure, thus maintaining the fiction of the LAC of 7 November 1959. India had consistently rejected the concept of a LAC both before and after 1962. From the Indian perspective, China was not physically present in areas that they claimed as lying on their side of the LAC. The actual ground positions of the two sides differed in several areas from the notional Chinese LAC. This posed a challenge. How could the two sides discuss the idea of peace and tranquillity in the border areas without having a common perception of where the two military forces were actually present in relation to each other in those areas? Without a common point of reference, it might have been practically difficult to ensure peace in the border region. Since the Sumdorong Chu stand-off was still unresolved in 1992, a common understanding on the actual ground position of the military forces of India and China was a pressing matter that needed addressing. With this in mind, the Indian side proposed to draw a distinction between the respective boundary claims of the two sides and their actual ground position in the border regions.[18] Doing so could enable India to discuss the actual ground situation in the border areas with a view to minimizing possible conflict, while retaining its claim to the entire territory. The Indian side was conscious that such an idea might give legal sanctity to the Chinese idea of an LAC, but there appeared to be no other possible way of finessing the matter at the time when the Indian side felt it desirable and on balance to have a more predictable border situation and to lower tensions with China in the border regions.

Negotiations, according to those who participated, were long and very hard.[19] The Chinese wanted to insert the term 'LAC of 7 November 1959' into the text of an agreement. The Indian side could not agree to such a reference in a bilateral agreement. This problem was sidestepped by inserting the provision that both sides would clarify the LAC wherever required,[20] which, by implication, meant that India did not share a common perception with China about the so-called LAC of 7 November 1959. There is no gainsaying that such a formulation did not conclusively reject the Chinese version of the LAC. But in the circumstances, the alternative might have been a continued state of close confrontation all along the LAC at a time when India was battling Pakistan-sponsored terrorism in both Punjab and Jammu and Kashmir. Choices had to be made and that is what India did. The resulting Border Peace and Tranquillity Agreement (BPTA) that was signed during Prime Minister Rao's visit in September 1993 not only formalized a commitment for both sides to respect the status quo, but also contained a provision to reduce military forces on the principle of 'mutual and equal security' and to work out confidence building measures in order to reduce the possibilities of military face-offs in the future. Foreign Secretary Dixit, who steered this agreement from the Indian side, later explained India's rationale for it. He wrote that the BPTA established a jurisdictional pattern regarding the LAC that would reduce the danger of unintended confrontation, because both sides felt it necessary to make moves on the LAC for tactical and counter-tactical reasons.[21] This agreement served the strategic requirements of India – a more predictable and peaceful northern border – for twenty years. The BPTA was the first agreement of its kind, specifically relating to our border region with China. In his address at Beijing University on 9 September 1993, Narasimha Rao struck an optimistic note when he said, 'Even on issues that once divided us, we are agreed on the need for and the manner of dealing with these questions. I am confident that if we both continue this process, our common border will continue to be a border of tranquillity'.[22]

The 1993 agreement became the basis on which both parties built the agreement between the Government of India and the Government of the People's Republic of China on Confidence Building Measures in the Military Field along the Line of Actual Control in the India-China Border Areas (known as CBMs). This second agreement was signed on 29 November 1996 during the visit of President Jiang Zemin to India. It not only declared that maintenance of peace and tranquillity along the LAC was in the 'fundamental interests of the two peoples', but also recognized that the full and proper implementation of CBMs depended on both sides arriving at a common understanding of the LAC (this had been India's point from the start). Both 'agree(d) to speed up the process of clarification and confirmation of the Line of Actual Control', including through an exchange of maps indicating their respective perceptions of the entire alignment of the LAC.[23] This agreement, thus, made India's divergence explicit with reference to the Chinese LAC of 7 November 1959, and also moved the needle on the urgency and importance of undertaking the task of clarifying the LAC. Any ambiguity in the 1993 agreement was thus resolved in 1996.

The Joint Working Group had already begun to work on identifying the possible areas of differing perceptions after resolving the prolonged stand-off in the Sumdorong Chu Valley in 1995. It has been claimed that both sides identified eight disputed 'pockets' along the LAC.[24] Once the 1996 CBM Agreement came into force, both sides agreed to expand this effort by exchanging maps of their respective perceptions of the LAC, beginning with the middle sector (the border with China in the states of Himachal Pradesh and Uttarakhand). This marked a significant step in the efforts to concretize measures to guarantee peace and tranquillity in the border regions. By March 2002, both sides had completed the exchange of maps of the middle sector and proceeded to the western sector (the border with China in the state of Jammu and Kashmir, and the Union Territory of Ladakh since August 2019). In June 2002 both showed their respective maps of the LAC alignment in the western sector to the other side, but there was no further progress in finalizing an exchange of maps in this sector. Maps of the eastern sector were neither shown nor exchanged. The reasons for the setback to the LAC clarification exercise have been the subject of speculation. Some experts have claimed that the stalemate happened because both countries had made maximalist claims to their respective LAC alignments.[25] One report, based on media sources, claimed that many more points of differing perceptions of the LAC alignment had emerged in the western sector as a result of the brief show-and-tell in June 2002, which made the map exchange unpalatable.[26] Despite efforts by the Indian side to bring negotiations back on track, the Chinese subsequently refused to resume the process of map exchanges that would have given both sides a clearer understanding of the other's perception. No Chinese writings have yet emerged in the public domain that lucidly explain their reasons for the about-turn. The argument about China being unhappy with India's depiction of the 'maximalist' position does not stand up to scrutiny. Each side had been given the freedom to depict the LAC according to its perception. There was no obligation on a party to accept the other side's claim depiction. The purpose of the exercise was merely to take note of possible areas of divergence along the LAC, which might be resolved through subsequent negotiations, or if that was not feasible, then 'managed' so that possibilities for conflict over the 'areas of differing perception' were minimized. Hence, it was only to be expected that both sides might show maximalist positions, and this cannot be a reasonable argument for reneging from an international agreement. There is a need to look elsewhere for the answers. It is possible that the Chinese side agreed to the LAC clarification exercise, on the presumption that they would be able to secure India's concurrence for their 7 November 1959 line. After all, the whole idea of the LAC was a Chinese one in the first place. If they were able to do that, the Chinese would have achieved two things: first, their possession of areas in the western sector (and other sectors) where they were not in actual control would be established, and second, because their LAC alignment in the western sector so closely mimicked their actual boundary claims, the Chinese would have effectively resolved the boundary in the western sector without an actual boundary negotiation. When India balked at endorsing the Chinese line, because it would have sanctioned their creeping attempts at changing facts on the ground, the Chinese seemed to lose interest in the process. India had demonstrated a genuine desire to stabilize and eliminate friction points all along the India–China border areas. The LAC clarification episode serves as a reminder that China might not fulfil treaty obligations if it does not suit China's interests.

After the strong momentum of positive relations in the early and mid-1990s, India's relations with China by 2001 had reached what Dixit called an 'inactive plateau'. In June 2003, India made another sincere effort to resolve the boundary question during the visit of Prime Minister Atal Bihari Vajpayee to China. Again, significant preparation went into this visit. In the Declaration on Principles for Relations and Comprehensive Cooperation between China and India that was concluded between Prime Minister Vajpayee and Premier Wen Jiabao on 23 June, they decided to 'each appoint a special representative (SR) to explore, from the political perspective of the overall bilateral relationship, the framework for a boundary settlement'.[27] The same document also iterated that neither side was a threat to the other, and that the common interests between them outweighed whatever differences existed. Brajesh Mishra was appointed as the first SR. His counterpart was Dai Bingguo, a seasoned party official with deep diplomatic skills. There were also some positive developments on complex political questions. The Indian side offered a more explicit recognition of Tibet as a part of the People's Republic of China in 2003, and the Chinese recognized Sikkim as a part of India in 2005.[28] The two countries even signed a memorandum of understanding on defence cooperation in May 2006, during the visit by Defence Minister Pranab Mukherjee, in order to build confidence and understanding between the militaries on both sides. The political initiative taken by India appeared to hold promise. Brajesh Mishra and Dai Bingguo agreed to a three-step process for the settlement of the boundary question. This three-step process consisted of first establishing the political parameters and guiding principles, which were to be followed by the evolution of a mutually acceptable framework, and ending with the delineation and demarcation of the boundary. They began a discussion on the structure of a new agreement that would lay down key principles and parameters as the basis for a final boundary settlement. The defeat of the NDA government at the electoral hustings less than one year later appeared to set back the process that both countries had begun for resolving the dispute. However, the new UPA government picked up the baton from its predecessor[*], and India's new government, led by Dr Manmohan Singh, and China signed the landmark Agreement on Political Parameters and Guiding Principles for the Settlement of the India–China Boundary Question during Premier Wen Jiabao's visit to India in April 2005. Regrettably, the 'symmetry of this consensus … proved to be short-lived', is how one former foreign secretary described it.[29] Both sides struggled to build on the momentum of 2005 and to deliver the second stage of the three-stage boundary settlement plan – drawing up a framework for the final settlement. Neither side has explicitly stated why a framework settlement continues to elude the negotiators.

---

[*] J.N. Dixit had returned as the national security advisor in 2004 to steer the talks on the boundary question, ten years after he had done so as the foreign secretary under Prime Minister Rao.

A partial explanation for the lack of success in reaching a mutually acceptable boundary settlement during the twenty years from 1992 to 2012 might lie in the 1993 and 1996 agreements themselves. In the process of their implementation, both India and China realized the backwardness of their infrastructure in the border areas. By making both sides more conscious of the importance of strengthening their physical presence in these areas, the two agreements might have inadvertently created conditions for the subsequent slowing down of the boundary negotiations until the parties felt they were in a more comfortable position along the LAC. China began modernizing its infrastructure in the border regions by the late 1990s and India followed suit. More permanent or semi-permanent military positions and posts sprang up closer and closer to the LAC, and the small number of direct contact points between the two sides correspondingly grew in consequence.[30] 'Face-offs' between the two sides became more frequent. Although both sides had developed protocols to handle such situations in a non-confrontational way, these measures were entirely voluntary and depended upon the good sense and restraint of local patrol leaders in tense situations. The 1993 and 1996 agreements had no provisions to enforce restraint upon either side. As a result, the border areas became 'live' to a greater degree than at any time since 1962. Managing the immediate situation along an increasingly active and yet undetermined LAC became the greater need, possibly putting the boundary issue on the back burner.

It is important to note that between 1990 and 2012 the initiatives to address long-pending issues in the relationship came primarily from the Indian side. This speaks to India's inclination to resolve difficult issues. Could the inability to solve the boundary question have had something to do with the lack of political will on the

Chinese side? China was focused on pursuing reformist domestic agendas and seeking Western assistance for its development in this period. Perhaps it was content to keep the relationship with India in neutral mode as it focused on more important priorities. There is reason to believe that India fell lower and lower in the list of Chinese foreign policy priorities during these twenty years, though the growth in bilateral functional ties created the illusion of a closer relationship. An astute observer of the relationship was to remark that the overt tensions that had marked India–China interactions had dissipated but latent suspicions had remained through the 1990s. This trust and information deficit could never be adequately bridged.[31] As a result of it, both managed their mutual competition or encouraged cooperation in areas where joint gains might be possible, but little was accomplished in the critical problems bedevilling the relationship.[32] China remained anxious over India's intentions regarding the Dalai Lama and the security of its Tibetan frontier with India. India was suspicious of China's strategic relationship with Pakistan and its implications for India's sovereignty and territorial integrity.

By the middle of the first decade of the twenty-first century, two fresh developments led to the deepening of suspicions that beset India-China ties. One concerned their common 'frenemy'– the United States of America. If in the early 1990s China felt that they might cooperate with India to limit American hegemony in the region,[33] by the late 1990s both China and India had begun to woo the Americans into supporting their strategic preferences over the other.[34] China's efforts to make common cause with the Americans, both during the CTBT negotiations and after the Indian nuclear tests in 1998, had caused unhappiness in India. India's claim that these tests had been in response to a Chinese nuclear threat were regarded by Beijing as groundless accusations intended to curry American favour. The second development after the year 2000 was the power asymmetry that developed after the Chinese economy took off. Between 2000 and 2010, China's comprehensive national power outstripped India's in terms of growth rates, actual GDP and military spending. China's GDP was roughly double that of India's in 2000. By 2010, it had grown to a factor of 4:1. These were also the years when China's diplomatic influence expanded, including in the regions surrounding India, and it came to expect that the West would accommodate its rise. Time appeared to be on China's side. China also began to outstrip India in terms of border infrastructure after 2005. In these circumstances, it is possible that the Chinese leadership may have felt no compelling reasons to settle the boundary question and were content with the status quo. This might also explain why all the initiatives for resolving the boundary question came from the Indian side in 1988 (Rajiv Gandhi), 1993 (P.V. Narasimha Rao) and 2003 (Atal Bihari Vajpayee). The Chinese might offer a different explanation for the stalemate on the boundary issue. They might claim that India was unwilling to make real 'adjustments' to the boundary by surrendering some of its territory in the eastern sector. There is an uncorroborated and anecdotal reference to the possible territorial expectations that China might have had.[35] This, however, cannot explain why they stalled the process of the LAC clarification. It is possible that the Chinese have all along felt that a commonly agreed LAC would harden into a de facto boundary over time, whereas China expected to gain territory in the final settlement and was content to delay it while it built up its relative power and advantage vis-à-vis India.

In many ways, the year 2005 was to be the high point in India–China relations in the post-Cold War period. Although the relationship continued to make progress on the surface even after 2005, it became apparent over the next few years that the consensus, outlined by the prime ministers of India and China in a joint statement in April 2005 (during the visit of Premier Wen Jiabao to India), was being adhered to by the Chinese side only when it suited them. Positive noises on bilateral trade and business continued to come out of Beijing because their exports gained greater and greater market share in India. On a range of matters of direct concern to India, however, including the clean 'waiver' for the Indo-American 123 Deal in the Nuclear Suppliers Group and the question of India's aspirations for permanent membership of the UN Security Council, the Chinese were ambivalent and worked behind the scenes to stall progress. On the Kashmir question, there was a brief period in the mid to late 1990s when China gave the appearance of adjusting its position by dropping references to the UN Security Council's role in resolving this matter. During the Kargil war, because India presented overwhelming proof of Pakistan's active involvement to the Chinese side, the Chinese took a more neutral stand in public. This was part of their effort to keep relations with India on an even keel. This ended after 9/11 and thereafter there was scant consideration for Indian sensitivities. Sino-Pakistani strategic relations continued to develop apace. Indeed, the Chinese appeared to have concluded that the improved relationship with India made it less problematic for them to continue their engagement with Pakistan. The Chinese provided nuclear-capable M-9 and M-11 missiles and missile technology to them and assisted Pakistan in its strategic programmes. Even when their attention was drawn to specific instances of Chinese assistance to Pakistan's nuclear weapons programme, such as the supply of dual-use ring magnets by China in 1995–96, the Chinese stoutly denied it – even after the Americans had shown them the evidence. The Defence Agreement signed in 2006 was intended to build trust between two of the world's largest standing armies. In 2009, China refused to issue a visa to India's Northern Army commander on the spurious argument that he exercised jurisdiction over territories that they claimed in Ladakh, which led India to question their sincerity on implementing even limited efforts at trust building. Even on the question of cooperation on shared rivers, after initially agreeing to exchange limited data for the Brahmaputra and Sutlej rivers, the expert-level mechanism stalled in its efforts to expand the effort to other common rivers, because the Chinese had changed their minds. For all China's talk about showing sensitivity to India's concerns, its actions post-2005 spoke louder than words. Meanwhile, India was asked to bend to Chinese sensitivities and to reiterate the 'one-China' policy in every major joint document. It also faced mounting pressure to accommodate Chinese concerns vis-à-vis His Holiness the Dalai Lama. The extraordinary security arrangements that China was able to obtain from India during the passage of the Olympic Torch in 2008, including the complete lockdown of central Delhi, the heart of the union government, marked, in one sense, the perigee in the relationship, which was now being seen as one-sided and unequal even by those who wanted better relations with China.

The backsliding was also visible on the boundary question. Within months of the Agreement on Political Principles and Guiding Parameters being signed in April 2005, China chose to reinterpret key provisions, especially Article 7, that referred to the 'safeguarding of due interests of settled populations in the border areas'. In May 2007, the Chinese foreign minister, Yang Jiechi, reportedly told External Affairs Minister Pranab Mukherjee that the mere presence of populated areas in Arunachal Pradesh would not affect the Chinese claims on the boundary.[36] From this point on, the efforts to find a framework settlement for the boundary question faltered, and over time the mechanism of special representatives was reduced to an annual consultation on foreign and security matters instead of a serious political initiative to resolve a long-standing dispute. More ominously, the Chinese official media began to refer to Arunachal Pradesh as 'South Tibet' after 2005. They signalled their intention by refusing to give a visa to an Indian government official who was serving in Arunachal Pradesh in late 2006. Subsequently, they started the practice of issuing 'stapled' visas – the visa was not affixed to the passport but was given on a separate piece of paper that was stapled to the passport – to all Indian citizens from Arunachal Pradesh (as well as from Jammu and Kashmir). By the end of 2009, the Indian side was left in no doubt that the Chinese were consciously seeking to emphasize the differences on the boundary question instead of narrowing them down. It was roughly from this time onwards that the LAC began to go 'live' once more.

One factor that appeared to hold great promise was the trade between India and China, which blossomed after the year 2000. Initially, both sides took satisfaction in the gross numbers that seemed to grow in geometric progression for a decade. Yet the dark truth was that here, too, a serious imbalance was emerging. In the year 2000, bilateral trade was around US $3 billion. By 2012 bilateral trade stood at an impressive US $66.47 billion, but the trade deficit was close to US $30 billion. The Indian side was also initially taken in by Chinese claims of investments worth US $60 billion, until it realized that the overwhelming majority of this was in terms of project exports in which no actual Chinese money was committed but large profits were generated for project execution by Chinese companies and the Chinese suppliers of goods and services required for the projects. Over time the widening trade deficit thus became a matter of serious concern for India. Each time a summit-level meeting took place, China's leaders assured India that they were conscious of trade concerns. Premier Wen always conveyed that China takes the issue of the trade deficit very seriously. On each such occasion, they would propose that the two commerce ministers should convene the Joint Economic Group in order to discuss the matter, but after the summit meeting the group would rarely meet. What could have become a significant binding force for the relationship became, after 2010, another problem because the Chinese side refused to address underlying Indian concerns despite repeated requests.

The Chinese side will claim that it was India, not China, that changed the paradigm of the relationship. This, according to them, was initially done when India raised the 'bogie' of the 'China threat' after the nuclear tests in order to ingratiate themselves with the Americans. They say that India joined hands with the United States in order to help 'contain' China. They draw a direct correlation between the warming of the India–US partnership after the conclusion of the Ten-Year Indo-US Defence Framework Cooperation Agreement and the initiation of the 123 Nuclear Deal in 2005, and the shift in China's India policy. The Chinese side claims that their policy changes were a reaction to these developments. Hence, these two allegations should be weighed carefully. With reference to the 'China threat', it is a matter of fact that Prime Minister Vajpayee made a factual reference to China in his letter to President Clinton after the Indian nuclear tests in May 1998, but it is equally true that China had continually helped Pakistan's strategic programmes after 1988, unmindful of Indian concerns that such weapons would be used against India. Sensitivity, it seemed, was unidirectional for China. What Prime Minister Vajpayee wrote in his letter to foreign leaders was an inconvenient truth that China wished to bury. With regard to the Chinese allegation that the warming India–US relationship was intended to 'contain' China, the truth is that the Indo-US partnership was, on any parameter of measurement, significantly less intense than that between China and America in the first decade of the twenty-first century. The likelier reason for Chinese concern was that it feared the emergence of India as a rival in Asia with American help. China has always found it difficult to accept parity with other Asian powers (including Japan). It considers itself to be the primary Asian superpower and is not willing to countenance India (or Japan) as another pole in the regional order. Their objective was to take India down a peg or two. Initially content in ensuring that this was achieved through relatively benign measures such as using proxies to agitate India's security concerns, including Pakistan and Bangladesh, to keep India preoccupied in South Asia, as well as by working against India in multilateral forums such as the CTBT negotiations, it became progressively more difficult after 2005 for China to balance its public posture of 'sharing space with India in Asia' with its actual policy of 'containment' once India became more aware of the Chinese game. By alleging that there was a growing strategic linking of India to the United States in an 'anti-China' alliance, it made it easier for China to justify why it was reneging on commitments and understandings that it had reached with the Indian leadership only a few years previously. It gradually became apparent that China was utilizing the various bilateral mechanisms more as window-dressing for demonstration effect than as effective platforms to build real cooperation. In areas of core strategic interest to India, they continued to dissimulate. As a result of such behaviour, by the end of the first decade of this century the illusion that the Chinese had wanted to maintain the common interests of India and China outweighing our differences was beginning to fray. In India, there was a growing feeling that a preponderance of congruence in interests between the two Asian countries might no longer be possible.

If India was aware by 2007–08 of the limitations of engagement with China, it is legitimate to ask why India continued with efforts to positively engage with China. The answer may lie in global geopolitics. Prior to 2009, much of the world, especially the Americans and more specifically the Indo-Pacific poles, including ASEAN, Japan and Australia, was in a hugely beneficial economic relationship with China. Politically, too, they required Chinese support to deal with the nuclear challenges in North Korea and Iran, as well as on the Afghanistan–Pakistan issue and the war on terror. Russia, India's traditional friend, was also steadily improving relations with China after the advent of President Putin, including by way of the transfer of sensitive military equipment to China. In our extended neighbourhood ASEAN, the Gulf Cooperation Council and the Central Asian republics were heavily dependent on the Chinese market. The international environment was not conducive to accommodate a more assertive Indian policy towards China. This was also the case with geo-economics. The 2000s were the decade in which the Chinese economy stole a march over the Indian economy. The resulting imbalance was exacerbated by the challenges that India faced after 2008 as a result of the Global Financial Crisis.

The Jiang–Hu period marked the first time that India had dealt in any meaningful way with the Chinese after the 1950s. It was a steep learning curve for India. The attempts at building a modus vivendi through the terms of eight Indian prime ministers[*] during this period may not have been entirely successful, but it

---

[*] Rajiv Gandhi, V.P. Singh, Chandrashekhar, P.V. Narasimha Rao, I.K. Gujral, H.D. Deve Gowda, Atal Bihari Vajpayee and Manmohan Singh

bought a quarter century of peace and tranquillity along the LAC and allowed India to focus on its economic development and growth. The easing of tensions with China also served a useful purpose during the decade of the 1990s when it was dealing with Pakistan's support for terrorism in the Punjab and expansionism in Jammu and Kashmir, especially in tempering Chinese support for Pakistan during the Kargil war. During this twenty-year period, all governments in India made sincere efforts to stabilize and advance ties with China.

:CHAPTER 8:

Conclusions

IN SOME WAYS, THE JIANG–HU PERIOD IS SIMILAR TO THE BRIEF REIGN OF the Yongzheng Emperor from 1722 to 1735. He was the fourth emperor of the Qing dynasty, which had ruled China from 1644 until 1911, and his brief reign was bookended by the two Qing emperors who are commonly regarded as great – Kangxi (1661–1722) and Qianlong (1735–96). Each had reigned for sixty years and the period they spanned, from 1661 until 1796, subsequently came to be called the KangQian Prosperous Era (*kangqian shengshi*). Except that there had been a third emperor between them – Yongzheng – whom few remember. It was almost as if his reign was an interregnum, a brief period of time between two great reigns, and yet his thirteen-year reign was filled with impressive administrative, financial and territorial accomplishments that would allow his son and successor, Qianlong, to expand the empire and take China to the highest point of its imperial power and prestige.[1]

Like Yongzheng, it might be the fate of Jiang Zemin and Hu Jintao to be bookended by two giants of the Chinese Communist Party – Deng Xiaoping and Xi Jinping. Like the KangQian Prosperous Era, the Deng–Xi period might be remembered as the time when China became prosperous and regained global power and position. And like the era of Yongzheng, the Jiang–Hu period might look like a time when the Chinese state was in a holding pattern until the next colossus came along. This, however, was not the reality. The reality was that in the twenty years between 1992 and 2012, China enjoyed its most productive period under the rule of the Chinese Communist Party. The two leaders pursued two key objectives – facilitating economic growth to eliminate poverty and develop a moderately prosperous society, and readying China to behave like a major power. Both had cut their political teeth in the 1950s and 1960s, and had learnt their politics under Deng Xiaoping. Both were party secretaries (Jiang in Shanghai and Hu in Tibet) during the tumultuous summer of 1989, and each had competently handled the political situation from the Party's perspective (in Hu Jintao's case, by the use of force). They drew the proper lessons from the Tiananmen Incident, preserving Deng's legacy of keeping the 'leftist' forces in the Party in check and putting the lid on mass campaigns and ideological struggles. Each focused on the economy, investing massively into the basic building blocks of infrastructure – roads, ports, high-speed rail and aviation – as well as in education, research and development. Jiang was relatively inexperienced in matters of foreign and national security policy but had Deng's steadying hand in his initial years in power after 1989. Hu was more experienced in national security and foreign policy matters because he had been the political commissar of the local PLA units during his time as Tibet's party secretary (1988–92), vice chairman of the Party and state's central military commissions from 1998 to 2005 and vice president of the People's Republic of China from March 1998 until he became president in March 2003.

Aside from the obvious achievements of the Jiang–Hu period outlined in the earlier chapters of this book, it was their skilful political handling of the challenges that marked them out. The reforms sometimes brought on unexpected or unanticipated problems that the Party had not faced in any earlier period, such as SOE reforms or the dismantling of the welfare system, and the two leaders thus had no earlier points of reference to fall back upon. They moved ahead on economic reforms by feeling the stones on the riverbed, just as Deng had said. When it threw up new challenges, like the need for raising new finances to fund the infrastructure they were building, the Party experimented with the monetization of land despite the clear political risks. Politically, they did not allow any sort of organized opposition against the Party (including cultural or semi-religious movements like Fa Lun Gong), but kept themselves open to those who might have new political ideas that could serve the Party within the unshakeable framework of its absolute leadership. They showed political dexterity by co-opting new elites or groups who had the potential to become future problems for the Party, such as the students or intellectuals, into the Party. They provided constitutional protection for non-state sector activities but retained control through the Party's mandatory units in such companies. They regulated the intellectual world, including the newly discovered internet, but did not stifle intellectual discourse on a broad range of subjects or deter scholars and researchers from having contact with foreigners and studying abroad. The age and term limits that Deng had introduced, the diffusion of power due to shared-by-differentiated responsibilities in the Party's highest organ – the

Politburo Standing Committee, and the absence of charisma all created an aura of normality that convinced the outside world that China was becoming a fully normal state.

Under Jiang and Hu, China's international image was also carefully crafted to project a non-threatening and benign power as it rapidly climbed up the international ranks. Both leaders avoided direct conflict with the US but assiduously worked to develop the tools to deny the Americans the capacity to 'contain' China. Each worked hard to shape China's image as a responsible and constructive power which would never seek hegemony or engage in power politics. The two used regional crises to effectively demonstrate that they were helping the region by building partnerships and facilitating solutions to dangerous problems like the nuclearization of North Korea. It was under their watch that China participated more actively in multilateral affairs from climate change to the Iran nuclear issue, demonstrating just enough independence to show themselves as a major power but without upsetting the American apple cart too much.[2] The demonstrations of unhappiness were carefully calibrated for the domestic audience and stopped before they created serious doubts about real Chinese intentions. The Party discovered that as China's power on the world stage grew, it could derive legitimacy from its defence of China's interests abroad after the mid-1990s, which Jiang Zemin encapsulated in a speech in 2001 on the eightieth anniversary of the Party's founding when he declared 'we have thoroughly ended the history of humiliating diplomacy in modern China and effectively safeguarded state sovereignty, security and national dignity'.[3]

Sometimes the Party stumbled and the mask briefly slipped, such as when Hu Jintao initially adopted the slogan of China's 'peaceful rise' that caused alarm and concern about Chinese intentions, especially in the region. Hu and the Party realized that the word 'rise' might sound like the Chinese were preparing to challenge the international order. It was quickly rectified by replacing the phrase with 'peaceful development', which took the menace out of it. A prominent Chinese scholar was to comment later: 'In substance, both peaceful rise and peaceful development carry the same message – that China's growing power will not be threatening to the outside world and, therefore, the many variations of the of the "China threat" theory are to be rejected'.[4] The international community largely bought the argument, just as they bought other carefully constructed matrixes to justify Chinese behaviour, including the so-called China threat theory, the idea of the 'Eastern NATO', the 'century of humiliation' (which was hardly unique to China in the Asian continent) and the concept that China would never seek hegemony. These ideas were developed and projected across the world by a legion of Chinese scholars and foreign policy experts who had gained unprecedented access to the West, and gave the Jiang–Hu administrations enough cover to build their military power and spread their influence in the region, by allowing China to sail below the radar in these years. The changes in the military were also very significant. Not only did Jiang and Hu encourage greater professionalization in the PLA, but, just as importantly, they displayed a long-term vision by building modern research and development infrastructure for weapons systems. These could produce an increasingly advanced suite of lethal weapons and enhanced China's military capabilities far quicker than anyone anticipated. It was on Hu's watch that the PLA also evolved new missions, including routine naval deployments to the Indian Ocean region. New training and exercise regulations with actual troops, real equipment and live ammunition drills became more common.[5] The 'Malacca Dilemma' resulted in the PLA beginning to make systematic investments into building platforms on the seas, in the air and in space, which would allow them to challenge American power in the Indo-Pacific after 2015. In almost every sphere of national endeavour, the Jiang–Hu period thus laid the groundwork and built the structure that would allow Xi Jinping to move China closer to the centre of the world stage.

The successes that Jiang and Hu chalked up had their consequences, and some of these became evident only towards the fag end of the period. The economy had grown so quickly that the Party struggled to keep up with all the changes. Policy differences could be handled in-house, but the reforms had also attracted interest groups who were vying for a bigger and bigger share of a rapidly expanding financial pie and were willing to use unconventional means to secure it. The scent of big money attracted the sharks – the red elite of China – and their cronies, who obstructed transparency, accountability and oversight as the reforms took root in China.[6] Some Chinese leaders had warned of this happening as early as 1996. Zhu Rongji is reported to have said, 'To fight corruption one must go after the tiger first, then the wolf. There will be absolutely no tolerance for the tiger. Prepare one hundred caskets and leave one for me. I am ready to perish in this fight if it brings the nation long-term stability and the public's trust.'[7] Zhu's advice went largely unheeded. Indeed, there are reports that his own family might have had deep interests in business and had benefitted from his high position. Lin Youfang, the wife of Jia Qinglin, a politburo member associated with the Shanghai Faction, was directly implicated in a massive US $6 billion smuggling operation by the Yuanhua group of companies. Rather than harming his career, Jia made it to the Politburo Standing Committee in 2007, thus demonstrating that the proper credentials and political allies bought protection against allegations of indulging in corrupt practices. Corruption, which had greased the wheels of the Chinese economy for over a decade, now threatened to clog the system like cancer. It ran so deep and became so pervasive by 2010 that it produced serious risk for the Party and the very stability of the Chinese political system that it had built.[8] Money was not being used simply for personal or family enrichment, but to secure power. It threatened to destabilize the political order. The Bo Xilai affair may have been the last straw.

The pace of fragmentation of its authority over its cadres was exacerbated by the dilution of the party's control and power over its military wing. The deal that Jiang and Hu had struck with the military – allowing them greater professional independence in return for accepting civilian control via their chairmanship of the Central Military Commission – had, over time, created power centres in the military and security forces. Theoretically, the politburo was the ultimate forum for approving key military appointments and decisions, but in practice, most military matters submitted to the politburo were automatically approved on the assumption that the Party's general secretary, who formally headed the Central Military Commission, had already green-lighted them. The CMC gradually became a more or less autonomous decision-making power, controlled by the two highest-ranking PLA leaders who took the positions of vice chairmen of this body. They decided on appointments and transfers, allocation of budgets, arms sales and purchases, and policy. The sale of military offices by the top echelons in the PLA became common by 2010. Corruption also seeped into the PLA. High-ranking members of the PLA, including the intelligence chief of the General Staff Department General Ji Shengde, were implicated in the Yuanhua corruption scandal.[9] Yet the investigations rarely yielded indictments and punishments of PLA personnel, because the Party's disciplinary bodies had lesser influence as compared to the PLA's in-house networks of money and power. By 2012, there were grounds to be concerned as to whether the basic adage of the Party – the gun is always under its control – was coming unstuck.

Inequalities in Chinese society as a result of economic growth also posed their challenges to the Party. The socio-economic changes in the twenty-year Jiang–Hu period were like nothing it had ever seen earlier. On the one hand, it had increased expectations within the general population. On the other, the relative freedoms and openness that the people now enjoyed made the inequities of the reform and the corruption within the Party more evident and perceptible. The extravagance and corruption among the cadres began to create distance between them and the general population and caused growing resentment. State monopolies and the privileges of the party elites became more blatant. Corruption was now perceived by the people as the greatest social evil. A party that at one time had made a revolution with the support of the people now seemed to have become a party of elites and vested interests that cared only for their future or, as one noted China scholar opined, that 'the gap between the fiction of the Party's rhetoric and the reality of everyday life grows larger every year.'[10]

In these circumstances, Bo Xilai's power grab marked the most serious political challenge that the Party faced within its ranks since the 1989 Tiananmen Incident. Bo's strong public campaign against evils like crime and corruption, his social welfare programmes, and his revival of the 'red culture', by using Mao-like slogans and campaigns to send his messages across, all made him genuinely popular with the public but it alarmed the elites. The fact that Bo Xilai was able to construct a popular political agenda associated with just his persona was unacceptable to the Party that had grown comfortable with the thought that the era of a single strongman had ended. Indeed, the Hu Jintao–Wen Jiabao duo that ruled China since March 2003 had been the most uncharismatic leaders since the Party had seized power in 1949. It had brought twenty years of political and social stability and the peaceful transition of power in 2002, and the Party was hoping for a similar transition in 2012. Bo was threatening to undo all this work to advance personal ambition and to divide the Party in the process, threatening the unity and solidarity that the rest had worked hard for in the past twenty years. After the murder of Heywood came to light and Wang Lijun fled to the American consulate in Chengdu, the Party faced a tense and uncertain situation as Bo Xilai fought to stay in power and the Hu–Wen duo sought to dislodge him. Major flaws in the communist political system came to light. The threats posed to the Party's grip on absolute power by factional politics, the patron–client ties based on money and power, the potential threat of ideological disunity as a result of Bo's 'leftist' rhetoric, and the public anger at the Party's corrupt actions all coalesced to spur them onto action. They selected Xi Jinping as the general secretary of China at the Eighteenth Party Congress in November 2012. Xi was a perfect counterfoil to Bo Xilai. Bo was over-exposed in the media; Xi was a relative enigma who had attracted limited public scrutiny even after twenty-five years in public life. Bo had been politically adventurous throughout his career, even using Maoist methods to further his political agenda; Xi was politically conservative. Bo was a flamboyant and in-your-face type of a leader; Xi associated himself with an earlier generation of communists who espoused hard work and plain living. Bo and his family made no secret of living well beyond their means; not even a hint of corruption had touched Xi Jinping. And since both were 'born red' (*zilaihong*), replacing one with another was something that the Party could live with if it helped to show unity and solidarity. It seemed that

Xi was made to order for a party that was flailing after two decades of unparalleled success.

Xi took office at a dangerous time in Chinese politics. To a world preoccupied by the Global Financial Crisis, the Chinese Communist Party appeared to the outside world as a cohesive and focused organization that had led China out of the crisis more successfully than other major economies, and had also ensured the smooth transition of power to the fifth generation of communist leaders. Yet Xi and his fellow leaders knew that China was politically brittle, the economy was still fragile and public credibility was at a low level. The Party was riven by factions and hooked on corruption. Although Xi had also become the chairman of the Central Military Commission, the military and security forces had gained enough autonomy to create doubts as to whether it would remain totally in the Party's control under any circumstances. In foreign policy terms, Deng's old formula appeared to have run its course, but the Party had no clear vision of what might replace it in a post-Global Financial Crisis world.[11] The question that Deng had posed in 1992, 'The problem now is not whether the banner of the Soviet Union will fall but whether the banner of China will fall?',[12] which the Party thought it had successfully thwarted after Tiananmen, returned to confront Xi and the new leadership at the end of 2012.

No single event has had such a major impact on the Communist Party of China than the disintegration of the Soviet Union. To understand the complete story of China's subsequent trajectory, including the one that it is following under Xi's leadership, it is necessary to understand the impact of the Soviet collapse.[13] It had deeply affected Xi Jinping. One of his earliest speeches, delivered secretly in January 2013 within two months of becoming the general secretary of the Chinese Communist Party, was about this topic. He was to say, 'To completely repudiate the history of the CPSU, to repudiate Lenin, to repudiate Stalin, was to wreck chaos in Soviet ideology and engage in historical nihilism. It caused Party organizations at all levels to have barely any function whatsoever. It robbed the Party of its leadership in the military. In the end, the CPSU – as great a party as it was – scattered like a flock of frightened beasts! The Soviet Union – as great a country as it was – shattered into a dozen pieces. This is a lesson from the past.' Xi amalgamated all that he thought was going wrong with his party in this analysis of what went wrong in the Soviet Communist Party – revisionism in party history, surrender of socialist ideology in the name of political reform, and loss of control over the military. He was determined to tackle the rot that he smelt in all these areas. Xi Jinping probably felt that he had no other choice other than to reassert central leadership and control over the Party and its instruments if it was not to go the eventual way of the Communist Party of the Soviet Union.

He tackled his party first. Xi highlighted the importance of cracking down on graft and corruption in his very first speech as the new general secretary of the Chinese Communist Party in December 2012. 'In this new environment, our Party is confronted with many severe challenges,' he said. 'There are many pressing problems within the Party that need to be resolved urgently, especially the graft and corruption cases that occurred to some of the party members and cadres ... '. In a subsequent speech, Xi said that failure to tackle the cancer of corruption 'will inevitably lead to the downfall of the Party and state' (*fubai zuizhong hui wangdang wangguo*). New rules of discipline for party members was one of his first actions. In December 2012, he announced an 'eight-point code' to guide the Party's behaviour.[14] On the ideological front, he began by restoring the centrality of the Party as the core of the political system. Document No. 9 (2013), 'On the Current State of the Ideological Sphere,' issued by the Party's central office, called for an all-out struggle against 'false ideological trends' like constitutional democracy, universal human rights, civil society, media and judicial independence and, most tellingly, questioning the inevitability of socialism in China under the Party's rule. It did not hesitate to identify the United States as the primary ideological threat to the Party's future as the ruler of China. To enforce his vision, Xi resorted to purges of a scale not seen after Mao, using the anti-corruption campaign that had already begun under Hu Jintao. He targeted big 'tigers', starting with Bo Xilai, the recently retired security czar Zhou Yongkang, believed to be a protégé of Jiang Zemin, and Ling Jihua, who was Hu Jintao's close political aide. All the power that had flowed downwards and outwards under Jiang and Hu began gradually to flow in the reverse direction.

Next, he tackled the military and security forces. He started his campaign of restoring the Party's complete control over PLA in November 2014 during the eighty-fifth anniversary of the Gutian Congress.[15] In November 2014, Xi reminded the PLA of this resolution, saying that it existed not simply to fight wars (that is, not just as a professional armed force), but it is an armed body for carrying out the political tasks of the Chinese revolution. He described the 'de-party-izing and depoliticizing' of the PLA as a Western way of subverting the Communist Party of China, and his first directive to the PLA was to rebuild the military's loyalty and ideological commitment to the Party. In a subsequent authoritative article, written by the PLA's General Political Department the following month, the phrase 'to scrape the poisoned tissues off bones' was used for the first time,[16] to hint at the use of harsh measures to enforce loyalty and purity. Weeks later Xi commenced his purge of the security forces by eliminating the influence of the two most powerful generals of the Hu-Jintao era – Guo Boxiong and Xu Caihou – to signal who was calling the shots from November 2012.

In domestic and foreign policies, Xi Jinping brought in new strategic frameworks. It likely stemmed from his assessment that the policy framework and economic strategy which had allowed China to experience unprecedented economic growth since 1978 had also resulted in deep structural imbalances and gross corruption that had tarnished the Party's claim to economic growth as the foundation for the regime's legitimacy.[17] Likewise, Deng's foreign policy of 'hide and bide' could not serve Chinese interests in the new situation when China was rising and needed to protect its overseas interests as well as guard against Western attempts to inhibit its rise. The focus shifted from quantitative numbers to qualitative indicators of economic progress, and new ways of doing business that would help China to ascend the value chain through innovation. In terms of foreign policy, the new approach was known as 'striving for achievement' (*fenfa youwei*), and emphasized a more proactive approach in which China would shape the international environment rather than simply integrate into it, and assert itself to confront threats rather than avoid the issue of conflict. At the beginning of his first term, his core objectives appeared to be no different from that of his predecessors. From Mao to Xi, they were united on the absolute principle that the Party had to remain in power, come what may. The world gave Xi the benefit of the doubt that he was cleaning up some of the problems of earlier administrations and his 'reign' would stay on the trajectory set by Jiang and Hu in the previous twenty years.

The Jiang–Hu interregnum has begun to fade from the public memory as 'Emperor' Xi has begun to govern in ways not anticipated either within China or by the rest of the world. As Xi identified and dealt with problems, both the Chinese Communist Party and the outside world showed understanding and patiently waited for the restoration of normalcy. In time, the list of problems from the earlier period grew large, while the achievements became fainter and disappeared from the public discourse. By the end of Xi Jinping's first term in office as general secretary of the Party in 2017, it seemed as if the great rejuvenation of the Chinese nation was entirely Xi's achievement, and owed little to his predecessors. Yet, the skilful handling of domestic politics by Jiang and Hu had allowed for twenty years of domestic social stability: the adept way in which the two conducted foreign policy to steer the Chinese ship in the direction of becoming a global influence while sailing mostly below the radar; the focused policy direction that allowed China to leapfrog in military technologies, to the point that its military is now able to challenge the main hegemonic power in large parts of the Indo-Pacific; the economic risks that Jiang and Hu took to create a US $11 trillion economy, which allowed China to come out of the Global Financial Crisis relatively unscathed; and the light touch that both exercised on intellectual and cultural controls, allowing for an explosion of ideas and innovation, has propelled the Chinese economy to becoming the world's largest. And this had all happened on the watch of Jiang Zemin and Hu Jintao. The interregnum might have been short in terms of time, but it was long in terms of productivity. These twenty years have many lessons for other developing countries – both positive and otherwise. It is also critical to our understanding of how China has risen and now dreams of global hegemony under Xi Jinping.

Acknowledgements

THE YEARS FROM 1990 TO 2010 MARKED MY MOST INTENSE ENGAGEMENT with China. I dealt with them in different capacities, and I owe a debt of gratitude to several colleagues who supervised my work during this time. Four, in particular, stand out for showing patience and for guiding me in improving my understanding – V.K. Nambiar, Shivshankar Menon, Nalin Surie and Neelam Sabharwal. I could consult them at any time and on any matter, and they were always free with their advice and opinions.

Carnegie India and its director, Rudra Chaudhary, who took me on board as a senior nonresident fellow, were helpful in providing access to material and digital sources that were immensely useful in writing this book, the more so because the pandemic made it difficult to access physical libraries or to meet with people. Carnegie India also provided me with a research assistant, Tisyaketu Sarkar, who tirelessly pored over books and notes and surfed the internet to track down material and information that I needed for this book. It would be no exaggeration to say that I would not have been able

ACKNOWLEDGEMENTS

to write this book without Tisyaketu's dogged efforts and never-give-up attitude to my endless demands.

Suchismita Ukil, who had edited my earlier book, *Tiananmen Square: The Making of a Protest*, approached the editing of this book with the same zeal and earnestness as the previous one. I owe Suchismita and the team at HarperCollins a debt of appreciation for their efforts to publish the book in record time.

These were the years during which my son, Jayant, followed us, mostly good-naturedly and uncomplainingly, between Beijing, Taipei and New Delhi as I pursued my diplomatic career. Our lives were shaped by our shared experiences. The first draft of this manuscript was written at the lovely home of Jayant and his wife, Sonali, in Seattle and, several months later, the final draft was also completed there. It is, therefore, only fitting that I dedicate this book to my son Jayant and his wife Sonali.

Of course, it goes without saying, my spouse Vandana remains the invisible hand behind all my writings on China.

Notes

Preface

1. Tone Tempest, 'China's Deng Xiaoping, 92, Dies,' *Los Angeles Times*, 20 February 1997.
2. *The Irish Times*, 21 February 1997

Chapter 1: Survival

1. Zhang Liang, eds. Andrew J. Nathan and Perry Link, *The Tiananmen Papers*, Little, Brown and Company, London, 2001, pp. 256–257.
2. Bao Pu et al, trans., *Prisoner of State: The Secret Journal of Zhao Ziyang*, Simon & Schuster, London 2009, pp. 247–253.
3. Document 9 a 'Communique on the Current State of the Ideological Sphere ‹was circulated by the General Office of the Communist Party's Central Committee in April 2013 that identified false ideological trends and activities including, inter alia, Western constitutional democracy, universal values, civil society, neo-liberalism, media freedom, historical nihilism, questioning the policy of reform, and opening up.

4. Bao Pu et al, trans, *Prisoner of State: The Secret Journal of Zhao Ziyang*, Simon & Schuster, London 2009, pp. 247–253.
5. Zhang Liang, eds. Andrew J Nathan and Perry Link, *The Tiananmen Papers*, Little, Brown and Company, London, 2001, pp. 308–314.
6. 'We Must Form a Promising Collective Leadership that will Carry out Reform,' 31 May 1989, *The Selected Works of Deng Xiaoping: Modern Day Contributions to Marxism–Leninism*, Vol. 3 (1982–1992).
7. 'Address to officers at the rank of general and above in command of troops enforcing martial law in Beijing,' 9 June 1989, *The Selected Works of Deng Xiaoping: Modern Day Contributions to Marxism–Leninism*, Vol. 3 (1982–1992).
8. Zhang Liang, eds. Andrew J Nathan and Perry Link, *The Tiananmen Papers*, Little, Brown and Company, London, 2001, pp. 431–436.
9. Li Peng's diary showed the top leadership closely watched developments. Martin K. Dimitrov, 'European Lessons for China: Tiananmen 1989 and Beyond,' chapter in *The Long 1989: Decades of Global Revolution*, Ed. Piotr H Kosicki and Kyrill Kunakhovich, Central European University Press (2019), pp. 61–88.
10. Gorbachev said, 'We deplore the turn of events.' – John Garver, 'The Chinese Communist Party and the Collapse of Soviet Communism,' *The China Quarterly*, No. 133 (March 1993), Cambridge University Press, pp. 1–26.
11. 'With stable policies of reform and opening up to the outside world, China can have great hopes for the future,' 4 September 1989, *The Selected Works of Deng Xiaoping: Modern Day Contributions to Marxism–Leninism*, Vol. 3 (1982–1992).
12. Arthur Waldron, 'Chinese Analyses of Soviet Failure: The Party,' *China Brief*, 2009, Vol. 9, Issue 23, The Jamestown Foundation.
13. Bao Pu et al, trans, *Prisoner of State: The Secret Journal of Zhao Ziyang*, Simon & Schuster, London, 2009.
14. Andrew J. Nathan and Perry Link, editors, *The Tiananmen Papers*, compiled by Zhang Liang, Little, Brown and Company, London, 2001, pp 338 -348. Excerpts from the State Security Ministry, 'On Ideological and Political Infiltration into our country from the

United States and other international political forces,' Report to Party Central, 1 June.

15. 'We are confident that we can handle China's affairs well,' 16 September 1989, *The Selected Works of Deng Xiaoping: Modern Day Contributions to Marxism-Leninism*, Vol. 3 (1982-1992).
16. 'We must adhere to socialism and prevent peaceful evolution towards capitalism,' 23 November 1989, *The Selected Works of Deng Xiaoping: Modern Day Contributions to Marxism-Leninism*, Vol. 3 (1982-1992).
17. John Garver, 'The Chinese Communist Party and the Collapse of Soviet Communism,' *The China Quarterly*, No. 133 (March 1993), Cambridge University Press, pp. 1-26.
18. Zhang Liang, eds. Andrew Nathan and Perry Link, *The Tiananmen Papers*, Little, Brown and Company, London, 2001, pp. 426-430.
19. John Garver, 'The Chinese Communist Party and the Collapse of Soviet Communism,' *The China Quarterly*, No. 133 (March 1993), pp. 1-26, Cambridge University Press.
20. 'The international situation and economic problems, 3 March 1990, to leading members of the Central Committee,' *The Selected Works of Deng Xiaoping: Modern Day Contributions to Marxism-Leninism*, Vol. 3 (1982-1992).
21. Richard Baum, 'Political Stability in Post-Deng China: Problems and Prospects,' *Asian Survey*, Vol. 32, No. 6 (June 1992), pp. 491-505, University of California Press.
22. Ezra Vogel, 'Deng's Finale: The Southern Journey,' *Deng Xiaoping and the Transformation of China*, Harvard University Press, 1992.
23. 'Seize the opportunity and develop the economy, 24 December 1990,' *The Selected Works of Deng Xiaoping: Modern Day Contributions to Marxism-Leninism*, Vol. 3 (1982-1992).
24. 'China will never allow other countries to interfere in its internal affairs, 11 July 1990,' *The Selected Works of Deng Xiaoping: Modern Day Contributions to Marxism-Leninism*, Vol. 3 (1982-1992).
25. Richard Baum, 'Picking Up the Pieces: Winter 1990 – Autumn 1991,' chapter in *Burying Mao: Chinese Politics in the Age of Deng Xiaoping*, Princeton University Press (1994), pp. 313-340.

26. Tony Saich, *From Rebel to Ruler: One Hundred Years of the Chinese Communist Party,* The Belknap Press of Harvard University Press, London, 2021, p. 317.
27. Richard Baum, 'Picking Up the Pieces: Winter 1990 – Autumn 1991,' chapter in *Burying Mao: Chinese Politics in the Age of Deng Xiaoping,* Princeton University Press (1994), pp. 313–340.
28. Suisheng Zhao, 'Deng Xiaoping's Southern Tour: Elite Politics in Post-Tiananmen China,' *Asian Survey,* August 1991, Vol. 33, No. 8, University of California Press, pp. 739–756.
29. Joseph Fewsmith, 'Reaction, Resurgence, and Succession: Chinese Politics since Tiananmen,' chapter in MacFarquhar, Roderick, *The Politics of China: Sixty Years of The People's Republic of China,* 2011, pp. 468–527.
30. Richard Baum, 'Picking Up the Pieces: Winter 1990 – Autumn 1991,' chapter in *Burying Mao: Chinese Politics in the Age of Deng Xiaoping,* Princeton University Press (1994), pp. 313–340..
31. Ezra Vogel, 'Deng's Finale: The Southern Journey,' chapter in *Deng Xiaoping and the Transformation of China,* Harvard University Press, 1992.
32. Excerpts from talks given in Wuchang, Shenzhen, Zhuhai and Shanghai, 18 January – 21 February 1992, *The Selected Works of Deng Xiaoping: Modern Day Contributions to Marxism–Leninism,* Vol. 3 (1982–1992).
33. Tai Ming Cheung, 'The PLA in 1992: Political Power and Power Projection,' *China Review,* 1993, Chinese University of Hongkong Press, pp. 6.1–6.21.
34. Gerald Segal, 'China and the Disintegration of the Soviet Union,' *Asian Survey,* Vol. 32, No. 9 (Sept 1992), University of California Press, pp. 848-868.
35. Excerpts from talks given in Wuchang, Shenzhen, Zhuhai and Shanghai, 18 January – 21 February 1992, *The Selected Works of Deng Xiaoping: Modern Day Contributions to Marxism–Leninism,* Vol. 3 (1982–1992).

Chapter 2: Quest for Prosperity

1. Wayne M. Morrison, US Congressional Research Service – 'China's Economic Rise: History, Trends, Challenges and Implications for the United States,' 17 December 2013.
2. Mary E. Gallagher, 'Reform and Openness: Why China's Economic Reforms Have Delayed Democracy,' *World Politics*, April 2002, Vol. 54, No. 3, Cambridge University Press, pp. 338-372.
3. A Speech at Fudan University, chapter in *Zhu Rongji on the Record – The Shanghai Years 1987–91*, 27 June 1988, Brookings Institution Press, 2018.
4. '"One Chop Zhu", Our Favourite Communist,' *The Independent*, UK, 19 June 1998.
5. Yingyi Qian, *How Reform Worked in China: The Transition from Plan to Market*, The MIT Press, 2017.
6. Jun Ma, *The Chinese Economy in the 1990s*, Palgrave Macmillan, London, 2000.
7. Lan Cao, 'Chinese Privatization: Between Plan and Market,' *Law and Contemporary Problems*, Vol. 63, No. 4, Public Perspectives on Privatization (Autumn 2000), pp 13-62, published by Duke University School of Law. Can be accessed at http://www.law.duke;edu/journals/63LCPCao.
8. Robert L. Kuhn, *How China's Leaders Think – The Inside Story of China's Reform and What it means for the Future*, John Wiley & Sons (Asia), Singapore, 2010.
9. Lan Cao, 'Chinese Privatization: Between Plan and Market,' *Law and Contemporary Problems*, Vol. 63, No. 4, Public Perspectives on Privatization (Autumn 2000), pp 13-62, published by Duke University School of Law. Can be accessed at http://www.law.duke;edu/journals/63LCPCao.
10. Yingyi Qian, '*How Reform Worked in China, The Transition from Plan to Market*,' The MIT Press, 2017.
11. Jack W. Hou, 'Economic Reform of China: Cause and Effects,' *The Social Science Journal 48* (2011), pp. 414–434.

12. Neil C. Hughes, 'Smashing the Iron Rice Bowl,' *Foreign Affairs* Vol. 77, No. 4 (Jul–Aug 1998), pp. 67–77.
13. Qin Gao, 'The Social Benefit System in Urban China: Reform and Trends from 1988 to 2002,' *Journal of East Asian Studies*, Vol. 6, No. 1 (Jan–Apr 2006), Cambridge University Press.
14. Kam Wing Chan, 'The Household Registration System and Migrant Labor in China: Notes on a Debate,' *Population and Development Review*, Vol. 36, No. 2 (June 2010), pp. 357–364.
15. Damien Ma, 'A Former Premier of China Speaks,' *The Atlantic*, 16 September 2011.
16. Li Cheng, 'China in 2000: A Year of Strategic Rethinking,' *Asia Survey*, Vol. 41, No. 1 (Jan/Feb 2001), University of California Press, pp. 71–90.
17. Mary E. Gallagher, 'Reform and Openness: Why China's Economic Reforms Have Delayed Democracy,' *World Politics*, Vol. 54, No. 3 (April 2002), Cambridge University Press, pp. 338–372.
18. Wenrong Jiang, 'Fuelling the Dragon: China's rise and its Energy and Resources Extraction in Africa,' *The China Quarterly*, No. 199 (Sep 2009), China and Africa: Emerging Patterns in Globalization and Development, Cambridge University Press for SOAS, pp. 585–609.
19. Roland Dannreuther, 'Asian Security and China's Energy Needs,' *International Relations of Asia-Pacific*, Vol. 3, No. 2 (2003), Oxford University Press, pp. 197–219.
20. Ziang Zemin's speech at luncheon by the American China Society and five other organizations, 30 October 1997.
21. Bill Clinton, *My Life*, Hutchison London, 2004, p. 768.
22. David Zweig, 'China's Stalled "Fifth Wave": Zhu Rongji's Reform Package of 1998–2000,' *Asian Survey*, Vol. 41, No. 2 (Mar–Apr 2001), pp. 231–247.
23. Bill Clinton, *My Life*, Hutchison London, 2004, p. 794.
24. Zhu Rongji, 'A Conversation with US Treasury Secretary Robert E Rubin, June 26, 1998,' chapter in *Zhu Rongji on the Record: The Road to Reform 1998–2003*, Brookings Institution Press.

25. Zhu Rongji, 'A Conversation with Alan Greenspan, Chairman, US Federal Reserve, January 12, 1999,' chapter in *Zhu Rongji on the Record: The Road to Reform 1998–2003*, Brookings Institution Press.
26. Joseph Fewsmith, 'The Politics of China's Accession to the WTO: Current History,' China, Vol. 99, No. 638 (Sep 2000), University of California Press, pp. 268–273.
27. ibid.
28. David Sanger, 'How Push by Chinese and US Business Won over Clinton,' *New York Times*, 15 April 1999.
29. Zhu Rongji, 'A Conversation with Pascal Lamy, EU Commissioner for Trade, March 29, 2000,' *Zhu Rongji on the Record: The Road to Reform 1998–2003*, Brookings Institution Press.
30. President Bill Clinton's speech at the Paul H. Nitze School of Advanced International Studies, Johns Hopkins University, as recorded by the Federal News Service, 9 March 2000.
31. Robert E. Scott, Report: 'Growth in US–China trade deficit between 2001 and 2015 cost 3.4 million jobs,' Economic Policy Institute, Washington, D.C., January 2017.
32. President Bill Clinton's speech at the Paul H. Nitze School of Advanced International Studies, Johns Hopkins University, as recorded by the Federal News Service, 9 March 2000.
33. Evan Feigenbaum, Damien Ma: 'China's Reform Imperative,' June 2014, Paulson Institute.

Chapter 3: Playing the West

1. David M. Lampton, 'China's Foreign Policy,' in *Great Decisions* (2014), Foreign Policy Association, pp. 73–84.
2. 'The Truth about US "Mediation" and the Future of the Civil War in China,' talk with the American correspondent A.T. Steele, 29 September 1949, *Selected Works of Mao Tse-tung*, Vol. IV.
3. 'On the People's Democratic Dictatorship: In commemoration of the twenty-eighth anniversary of the Communist Party of China, 30 June 1949,' *Selected Works of Mao Tse-tung*, Vol. IV.

NOTES

4. Memoirs of Chinese Finance Minister Bo Yibo, excerpt on 'Peaceful Evolution', 1991, History and Public Policy Program Digital Archive, Bo Yibo, *Ruogan zhongda juece yu Shijian de huigu* (Recollections of Several Important Political Decisions and Their Implementation), Zhonggong Zhongyang Dangxiao Chubanshe, Beijing, 1991. Can be accessed at http://digitalarchive.wilsoncenter;org/document/117029.
5. 'We are confident that we can handle China's affairs well, 16 September 1989,' *The Selected Works of Deng Xiaoping: Modern Day Contributions to Marxism–Leninism*, Vol. 3 (1982–1992).
6. 'The US should take the initiative in putting an end to the strains in Sino-American relations, 31 October 1989,' *The Selected Works of Deng Xiaoping: Modern Day Contributions to Marxism–Leninism*, Vol. 3 (1982–1992).
7. 'With Stable Policies of Reform and Opening up to the Outside World, China Can have Great Hopes for the Future, 4 September 1989,' *The Selected Works of Deng Xiaoping: Modern Day Contributions to Marxism–Leninism*, Vol. 3 (1982–1992).
8. 'The International Situation and Economic Problems, 3 March 1990,' *The Selected Works of Deng Xiaoping: Modern Day Contributions to Marxism–Leninism*, Vol. 3 (1982–1992).
9. John Garver, 'The Chinese Communist Party and the Collapse of Soviet Communism,' *The China Quarterly*, No. 133 (March 1993), Cambridge University Press, pp. 1–26.
10. 'Seize the Opportunity to develop the Economy, 24 December 1990,' *The Selected Works of Deng Xiaoping: Modern Day Contributions to Marxism–Leninism*, Vol. 3 (1982–1992).
11. Allen S. Whiting, 'Chinese Nationalism and Foreign Policy After Deng,' *The China Quarterly*, No. 142 (June 1995), Cambridge University Press on behalf of SOAS, pp. 295–316.
12. J. Stapleton Roy and Charles Kraus, 'The Communist Domino That Would Not Fall: China's Resilience at the End of the Cold War,' *The Wilson Quarterly*, Fall 2016, Woodrow Wilson International Center for Scholars.

13. You Ji, 'The PLA, CCP and Formulation of China's Defence and Foreign Policy,' chapter in eds. Yongjin Zhang and Greg Austin, *Power and Responsibility in Chinese Foreign Policy*, , Australian National University (ANU) Press.
14. Tony Saich, *From Rebel to Ruler: One Hundred Years of the Chinese Communist Party*, The Belknap Press of the Harvard University Press, London, 2020.
15. Full Text of Speech is available at https://asiasociety.org.
16. Bill Clinton, *My Life*, Hutchison, London, 2004, p. 768.
17. The speech by President Lincoln at the dedication of the national cemetery on the site of the battle of Gettysburg on 19 November 1863, where Lincoln spoke of 'government of the people, by the people, for the people'.
18. China–US joint statement, 29 October 1997.
19. Joseph Fewsmith, *China since Tiananmen: From Deng Xiaoping to Hu Jintao*, Cambridge University Press, 2001, 2008.
20. Gregory J. Moorer, 'Not Very Material but Hardly Immaterial, China's Bombed Embassy and Sino-American Relations,' *Foreign Policy Analysis*, January 2010, Vol. 6, No. 1, pp. 23–41.
21. Mario Esteban, 'The Management of Nationalism During the Jiang Era (1994–2002) and Its Implications on Government and Regime Legitimacy,' *European Journal of East Asian Studies*, Vol. 5, No. 2 (2006), Brill, pp. 181–214.
22. Allen S. Whiting, 'Chinese Nationalism and Foreign Policy After Deng,' *The China Quarterly*, June 1995, No. 142, Cambridge University Press on behalf of SOAS, pp. 295-316 .
23. Suisheng Zhao, 'Chinese Nationalism and its International Orientations,' *Political Science Quarterly*, Vol. 115, No. 1 (2000); and Jia Qingguo, 'Disrespect and Distrust: The External Origins of Contemporary Chinese Nationalism,' *Journal of Contemporary China*, 14:42, 11–21, DOI: 10.1080/1067056042000300754, pp. 1–33.
24. C. Schnellbach and Joyce Man, 'Germany and China: Embracing a Different Kind of Partnership?' Cap working paper, September 2015, Centre for Applied Policy Research, Munich University.

25. E. Sandschneider, 'China's Diplomatic Relations with States of Europe,' *The China Quarterly*, No. 169 (March 2002), Special Issue – China and Europe since 1978: A European Perspective, Cambridge University Press for the School for Oriental and African Languages, pp. 33–44.
26. 'How Germany Opened the Door to China and Threw away the Key,' *Politico*, 10 September 2020.
27. Hans Kundnani and Jonas Parello-Plesner, *China and Germany: Why the Emerging Special Relationship Matters for Europe*, European Council of Foreign Relations, May 2012.
28. John Fox and Francois Godement, *A Power Audit of EU-China Relations*, European Council of Foreign Relations, April 2009.
29. Xinning Song, 'Challenges and Opportunities in European Union–China Relations,' chapter in ed. Roland Vogt, *Europe and China: Strategic Partners or Rivals?*, Hong Kong University Press.
30. C. Schnellbach and Joyce Man, 'Germany and China: Embracing a Different Kind of Partnership?,' CAP working paper, September 2015, Centre for Applied Policy Research, Munich University.
31. 'The International Situation and Economic Problems, 3 March 1990,' *The Selected Works of Deng Xiaoping, Modern Day Contributions to Marxism–Leninism*, Vol. 3 (1982–92).
32. Nick Norling, 'China and Russia: Partners with Tensions,' *Policy Perspectives*, Vol. 4, No. 1 (Jan–Jun 2007), Pluto Journals, pp. 33–48.
33. Michael C. Chase, Evan Medeiros et al, 'Russia-China Relations, Assessing Common Ground and Strategic Fault Lines,' The National Bureau of Asian Research, NBR Special Report #66, July 2017.
34. Evan Medeiros, 'China's Foreign Policy Outlook,' chapter in *China's International Behaviour, Activism, Opportunism and Dynamism*, Rand Corporation.
35. Rush Doshi, 'Hu's to Blame for China's Foreign Assertiveness?,' chapter in Global China: Assessing China's Growing Role in the World, eds. Tarun Chhabra, Rush Doshi et al, Brookings Institution Press (2021), pp. 25–32.

36. Xiao Xiongyi, 'Chinese Foreign Policy in Transition: Understanding China's "Peaceful Development"', *The Journal of East Asian Affairs*, Vol. 19, No. 1 (Spring/Summer 2005), Institute for National Security Studies (INSS), pp. 74–112.
37. Zheng Bijian, 'China's Peaceful Rise and the Future of Asia and The New Path of China's Peaceful Rise and Sino-US Relations,' article in Documenting China: A Reader in Seminal Twentieth Century Texts, Hillenbrand, Margaret and Chloe Starr (eds.), University of Washington Press 2011, pp. 215–31.
38. Bonnie Glaser and Evan Medeiros, 'The Changing Ecology of Foreign Policy Making in China: The Ascension and Demise of the Theory of Peaceful Rise,' *The China Quarterly*, No. 190 (June 2007), Cambridge University Press on behalf of SOAS, pp. 291–310.
39. You Ji, 'The PLA, CCP and the formulation of China's Defence and Foreign Policy,' chapter in *Power and Responsibility in China's Foreign Policy*, eds. Yongjin Zhang and Greg Austin, Chapter: ANU Press.
40. Yan Xuetong, 'From Keeping a Low Profile to Striving for Advancement,' *The Chinese Journal of International Politics*, 2014, pp. 153–184.

Chapter 4: Wooing the Rest

1. David M. Lampton, 'China's Foreign Policy,' in *Great Decisions* (2014), Foreign Policy Association, pp. 73–84.
2. M. Swaine and A. Tellis, *Interpreting China's Grand Strategy*, Santa Monica, Calif: RAND Corporation 2000, p. 137.
3. Alice D. Ba, 'China & ASEAN: Renavigating Relations for a 21st Century Asia,' *Asian Survey*, 43:4, 2003, University of California, Berkeley, pp. 622–647.
4. Bruce Vaughn and Wayne Morrison, 'China–South-East Asia Relations: Trends, Issues and Implications for the United States,' CRS Report for Congress, 4 April 2006.
5. Valerie Niquet, 'China and Central Asia,' trans. Nick Oates, *China Perspectives*, Issue No. 67 (Sep–Oct 2006), Centre d'etude francais sur la Chinese contemporarie.

6. Wenrong Jiang, 'Fuelling the Dragon: China's Rise and its Energy and Resource Extraction in Africa,' *The China Quarterly*, No. 199, Sep 2009; and Julia C. Strauss and Martha Saavedra, China and Africa: Emerging Patterns in Globalization and Development, Cambridge University Press, pp. 585–609.
7. Michal Meidan, 'China's Africa Policy: Business Now, Politics Later,' *Asian Perspective*, Vol. 30, No. 4 (2006), Special Issue on Rising China's Foreign Relations, pp. 69–93.
8. Wenrong Jiang, 'Fuelling the Dragon: China's Rise and its Energy and Resource Extraction in Africa,' *The China Quarterly*, No. 199, Sep 2009; and Julia C. Strauss and Martha Saavedra, China and Africa: Emerging Patterns in Globalization and Development, Cambridge University Press, pp. 585–609.
9. Lloyd Thrall, 'China's Presence and Behaviour in Africa,' *China's Expanding Africa Relations*, Rand Corporation.
10. Roland Dannreuther, 'Asian Security and China's energy Needs,' *International Relations of Asia-Pacific*, Vol. 3, No. 2 (2003), Oxford University Press, pp. 197–219.
11. Chen Shaofeng, 'Has China's Foreign Energy Quest Enhanced its Energy Security?,' *The China Quarterly*, No. 207 (Sep 2011), Cambridge University Press for SOAS, pp. 600–625.
12. ibid.
13. ibid.
14. Michael T. Klare, 'Fuelling the Dragon: China's Strategic Energy Dilemma,' *Current History*, Vol. 105, No. 690. The Rise of Asia (Apr 2006), University of California Press, pp. 180–185.
15. Lloyd Thrall, 'China's Presence and Behaviour in Africa,' chapter in *China's Expanding Africa Relations*, Chapter: Rand Corporation.
16. A. Scobell and Alireza Nader, *China in the Middle East: The Wary Dragon*, RAND Corporation 2016.

NOTES

Chapter 5: The Malacca Dilemma

1. Sheryl Wudunn, 'China Browses for Tanks, Aircraft and Carriers in ex-Soviet Lands,' *New York Times*, 7 June 1992, p. 20.
2. Minnie Chan, 'Mission Impossible: How One Man Bought China its First Aircraft Carrier,' *South China Morning Post*, 19 January 2015.
3. A.A. Sergounin and S.V. Subbotin, SIPRI Research Report No. 15, Russian Arms Transfers to East Asia in the 1990s, Oxford University Press (1999).
4. Ian Storey, You Ji, 'China's Aircraft Carrier Ambitions,' *Naval War College Review* (2004), Vol. 57, No. 1 Winter, Article 8, pp. 1–18.
5. Minnie Chan, 'The Inside Story of the Liaoning: How Xu Zenping Sealed the Deal for China's First Aircraft Carrier,' *South China Morning Post*, 19 January 2015.
6. Ian Storey, You Ji, 'China's Aircraft Carrier Ambitions,' *Naval War College Review* (2004), Vol. 57, No. 1 Winter, pp. 1–18.
7. Sheryl Wudunn, 'China Browses for Tanks, Aircraft and Carriers in ex-Soviet Lands,' *New York Times*, 7 June 1992, p. 20.
8. V.M. Zubok, trans., First Conversation between N.S. Khrushchev and Mao Zedong, Hall of Huaizhentan (Beijing), 31 July 1958, History and Public Policy Program Digital Archive, Archive of the President of the Russian Federation, fond 52, opis 1, delo 498, ll. 44-477, copy in Dmitry Volkogonov Collection, Manuscript Division, Library of Congress, Washington, D.C., https://digitalarchive.wilsoncenter.org/document/112080
9. Jun Zhan, 'China goes to the Blue Waters: The Navy, Seapower Mentality and the South China Sea', *Journal of Strategic Studies*, Routledge, pp. 180–208.
10. Ian Storey, You Ji, 'China's Aircraft Carrier Ambitions,' *Naval War College Review* (2004), Vol. 57, No. 1 Winter, pp. 1–18.
11. Lee Jae-Hyung, 'China's Expanding Maritime Ambitions in the Western Pacific and Indian Ocean,' *Contemporary South-East Asia*, Vol. 24, No. 3 (Dec 2002), ISEAS pp. 549–568.

12. Ian Storey, You Ji, 'China's Aircraft Carrier Ambitions,' *Naval War College Review* (2004), Vol. 57, No. 1 Winter, pp. 1–18.
13. Lee Jae-hyung, 'China's Expanding Maritime Ambitions in the Western Pacific and the Indian Ocean,' *Contemporary Southeast Asia*, Vol. 24, No. 3 (Dec 2002), ISEAS, pp. 549–568. In August 2000, Tianma Shipbreaking of Tianjin bought the *Kiev* for scrap and in September 2000 China bought the carrier *Minsk* from South Korea as a tourist attraction.
14. Daniel J. Kostecka, 'PLA Doctrine and the Employment of Sea-based Airpower,' *Naval War College Review*, Vol. 64, No. 3 (summer 2011), US Naval War College Press, pp. 10–30.
15. Howard J. 'Dooley, The Great Leap Outward: China's Maritime Renaissance,' *The Journal of East Asian Affairs*, Spring/Summer 2012, Vol. 26, No. 1, Institute for National Security Strategy, pp. 53–76.
16. Jun Zhan, 'China Goes to the Blue Waters, The Navy, Seapower Mentality and the South China Sea,' *Journal of Strategic Studies*, Routledge London, pp. 180–208.
17. *Law of the Sea: A Policy Primer*, The Fletcher School, Tufts University, 2016.
18. 'China Adheres to the Position of Settling Through Negotiation the Relevant Disputes between China and the Parties in the South China Sea,' China White Paper, 13 July 2016.
19. Ji Guoxing, 'China versus South China Sea', No. 1 (1998), *Security Dialogue* 29, pp. 101–112.
20. Ian Storey, You Ji, 'China's Aircraft Carrier Ambitions,' *Naval War College Review* (2004), Vol. 57, No. 1 Winter, pp. 1–18.
21. Cheng Hurng-Yu, 'The PRC's South China Sea Policy and Strategies of Occupation in the Paracel and Spratly islands', *Issues and Studies* 36, No. 4 (July/August 2000), pp. 95–131.
22. Lee Lai To, 'China, the USA and the South China Sea Conflicts', *Contemporary Southeast Asia* 33, No. 3(Dec 2011), pp. 292–319.
23. Wu Shicun and Ren Huaifeng, 'More Than a Declaration: A commentary on the background and the significance of the

Declaration on the Conduct of the Parties in the South China Sea', *Chinese Journal of International Law* (2003), pp. 311–319.
24. Angus Maddison, *The World Economy: Historical Statistics*, Development Centre of OECD, 2003, p. 261.
25. Martin Stuart Fox, *A Short History of China and South-East Asia: Tribute, Trade and Influence*, Allen & Unwin, Australia, 2003, pp. 26–36.
26. Martin Stuart Fox, *A Short History of China and South-East Asia: Tribute, Trade and Influence*, Allen & Unwin, Australia, 2003, pp. 73–93.
27. Nicholas Tarling, *Cambridge History of South-East Asia: From Early Times to c. 1800*, Vol. 1, Cambridge University Press, 1992.
28. Zhongxiang Zhang, 'China's Energy Security, the Malacca Dilemma and Responses,' *Energy Policy*, Elsevier 2011.
29. You Ji, 'Dealing with the Malacca Dilemma: China's Effort to Protect its Energy Supply,' *Strategic Analysis*, Vol. 31, No. 3 (May 2007), Routledge, pp. 467–489.
30. ibid.
31. Chen Shaofeng, 'China's Self Extraction from the Malacca Dilemma and its Impact on ASEAN,' *International Journal of China Studies*, Vol. 1, No. 1 (Jan 2010), University of Malaya, Malaysia, pp. 1–24.
32. Marc Lanteigne, 'China's Maritime Security and the "Malacca Dilemma",' *Asian Security*, Vol. 4, 2008 – Issue 2.
33. You Ji, 'Dealing with the Malacca Dilemma: China's Effort to Protect its Energy Supply,' *Strategic Analysis*, Vol. 31, No. 3 (May 2007), Routledge, pp. 467–489.
34. Li Jian, Chen Wenwen and Jin Chang, 'Strategic Maritime Situation in the Indian Ocean and the Expansion of Chinese Maritime Power,' *Pacific Journal*, May 2014.
35. *The Chinese Navy: Expanding Capabilities, Evolving Roles*, Center for Study of Chinese Military Affairs, Institute for National Strategic Studies, National Defence University, Washington DC, (2008); and Du Chaoping and Liang Guihua: 'India Builds a New Far Eastern Strategic Defence Base', *Dang Hai Haijun*, No. 4 (2004).

36. You Ji, 'Dealing with the Malacca Dilemma: China's Effort to Protect its Energy Supply,' *Strategic Analysis*, Vol. 31, No. 3 (May 2007), Routledge, pp. 467–489.
37. Andrew Erickson and Lyle Goldstein, 'Gunboats for China's new Grand Canals? Probing the Intersection of Beijing's Oil and Security Policies,' *Naval War College Review*, Vol. 62, No. 2 (Spring 2009), US Naval War College Press, pp. 43–76.
38. Nan Li, C. Weuve, 'China's Aircraft Carrier Ambitions: An Update,' *Naval War College Review*, Vol. 63, No. 1 (Winter 2010), pp. 12–32.
39. 'The Chinese Navy: Expanding Capabilities, Evolving Roles,' Center for Study of Chinese Military Affairs, Institute for National Strategic Studies, National Defence University, Washington, D.C., 2008.
40. Bernard D. Cole, 'Rightsizing the Navy: How Much Naval Force will Beijing Deploy?,' chapter in *The Chinese Navy: Expanding Capabilities, Evolving Roles*, 2008, Center for Study of Chinese Military Affairs, Institute for National Strategic Studies, National Defence University, Washington, D.C., pp. 523–556.
41. Fravel and Libermann, 'Beyond the Moat – Evolving Interests and Influence,' chapter in *The Chinese Navy: Expanding Capabilities, Evolving Roles*, 2008, Center for Study of Chinese Military Affairs, Institute for National Strategic Studies, National Defence University, Washington, D.C.
42. Stratfor, Global Intelligence, Special Series: The Chinese Navy, April 2, 2009, www.stratfor.com
43. Michael McDevitt, Kamphausen and A. Scobell (eds.), 'The Strategic and Operational Context Driving PLA Navy Building,' chapter in *Rightsizing the PLA: Exploring the Contours of China's Military*, September 2007, Strategic Studies Institute, US Army War College, pp. 481–522.
44. Jayadeva Ranade, *China Unveiled: Insights into Chinese Strategic Thinking*, KW Publishers Pvt. Ltd, New Delhi (2013), pp. 101–109.
45. 'How China Developed its Defence Industry?,' China Power Project, Center for Strategic & International Studies (CSIS), 2021.

46. Evan Medeiros, Roger Cliff et al, 'A New Direction for China's Defense Industry,' Rand Corporation, Project Air Force, 2005.
47. 'How China Developed its Defence Industry?,' China Power Project, Center for Strategic & International Studies (CSIS), 2021.
48. Roy Kampenhausen, David Lai and Travis Tanner (eds.), *Assessing the PLA in the Hu Jintao Era*, The Strategic Studies Institute, US Army War College Press, April 2014.
49. Editorial, *PLA Liberation Army Daily*, 1 October 2005.
50. James Mulvenon, 'Chairman Hu and the PLA's New Historic Missions,' *China Leadership Monitor* No. 27.
51. James Mulvenon, Rebecca Samm Tyroler-Cooper, 'China's Defence Industry on the Path of Reform,' prepared for the US-China Economic & Security Review Commission, October 2009.
52. Yin Chengde, 'New Posture of US Asia-Pacific Strategy,' 10 *China International Studies*, 41 (2008).
53. Zhao Qinghai, 'The Four Nation Alliance: Concept versus Reality,' 9 *China International Studies* 11 (2007).
54. Chu Shulong, 'The Security Challenges in North-East Asia: East Asian Security,' in *Two Views*, Chu Shulong and Gilbert Rozman, Strategic Studies Institute, US Army War College (2007).
55. Yang Jiechi's speech at the Asia Society in Melbourne on 13 December 2005.

Chapter 6: The Party Means Business

1. In China the party secretary ranks higher than the governor of a province or the mayor of a city in deference to the Party's superior status vis-à-vis the State.
2. The 'eight immortals' were Deng Xiaoping, Chen Yun, Yang Shangkun, Wang Zhen, Li Xiannian, Peng Zhen, Bo Yibo and Song Renqiong, all of whom played pivotal political roles in post-Cultural Revolution China.
3. Yuen Yuen Ang, *China's Gilded Age: The Paradox of Economic Boom and Vast Corruption*, Cambridge University Press (2020), pp. 125–136.

NOTES

4. Jayadeva Ranade, *Xi Jinping's China*, KW Publishers Pvt. Ltd (2018), pp. 14–28.
5. Tony Saich, *From Rebel to Ruler: One Hundred Years of the Chinese Communist Party*, The Belknap Press of Harvard University Press, London (2021).
6. It was claimed that she had forced cyanide down the throat of an intoxicated Neil Heywood and left him to die alone. Source: Kerry Brown, *The New Emperors, Power and Princelings in China*, I.B. Tauris & Co. Ltd, London (2014).
7. Jayadeva Ranade, *Xi Jinping's China*, KW Publishers Pvt. Ltd (2018), pp. 14–28.
8. His supporters included Zhou Yongkang, the man who controlled the entire national security apparatus, and elements of the PLA such as the 13th and 14th Group armies, who were all subsequently purged by Xi Jinping. Source: Jayadeva Ranade, *Xi Jinping's China*, KW Publishers Pvt. Ltd (2018), pp. 14–28.
9. Yuen Yuen Ang's *China's Gilded Age* (CUP, 2020) is recommended for detailed understanding of this transition.
10. Tony Saich, *From Rebel to Ruler: One Hundred Years of the Chinese Communist Party*, The Belknap press of Harvard University Press, London (2021).
11. Damien Ma, 'A Former Premier of China Speaks,' *The Atlantic*, 18 September 2011.
12. Tony Saich, *From Rebel to Ruler: One Hundred Years of the Chinese Communist Party*, The Belknap press of Harvard University Press, London (2021).
13. Yuen Yuen Ang, *China's Gilded Age: the Paradox of Economic Boom and Vast Corruption*, Cambridge University Press (2020).
14. Richard Smith, 'Guanxi and the Game of Thrones, Wealth, Prosperity and Insecurity in a Lawless System,' in *China's Engine of Environmental Collapse*, Pluto Press (2020).
15. Yuen Yuen Ang, *China's Gilded Age: the Paradox of Economic Boom and Vast Corruption*, Cambridge University Press (2020).

16. Richard Smith, 'Guanxi and the Game of Thrones, Wealth, Prosperity and Insecurity in a Lawless System,' in *China's Engine of Environmental Collapse*, Pluto Press (2020).
17. Yuen Yuen Ang, *China's Gilded Age: the Paradox of Economic Boom and Vast Corruption*, Cambridge University Press (2020).
18. Kerry Brown, *The New Emperors: Power and Princelings in China*, I.B. Tauris & Co. Ltd, London (2014).
19. Richard Smith, 'Guanxi and the Game of Thrones, Wealth, Prosperity and Insecurity in a Lawless System,' in *China's Engine of Environmental Collapse*, Pluto Press (2020).
20. Kerry Brown, *The New Emperors: Power and Princelings in China*, I.B. Tauris & Co. Ltd, London (2014).
21. Damien Ma, 'A Former Premier of China Speaks,' translated excerpts from the book of speeches by Zhu Rongji, *The Atlantic*, 15 September 2011.
22. Yuen Yuen Ang, *China's Gilded Age: the Paradox of Economic Boom and Vast Corruption*, Cambridge University Press (2020).
23. Richard Smith, 'Guanxi and the Game of Thrones, Wealth, Prosperity and Insecurity in a Lawless System,' in *China's Engine of Environmental Collapse*, Pluto Press (2020).
24. 'The New Lap of Luxury, Global Retail and Consumer Products,' Ernst & Young China, September 2005.
25. Robert Kuhn, *How China's Leaders Think: The Inside Story of China's Reform and What it Means for the Future*, John Wiley & Songs (Asia) Pvt Ltd, Singapore (2010).
26. The Three Represents was Jiang Zemin's ideological contribution to Chinese socialism. It averred that the Party must support the development of productive forces, advancement of Chinese culture and the fundamental interest of the Chinese people.
27. Richard McGregor, *The Party: The Secret World of China's Communist Rulers*, HarperCollins (2010).
28. Tony Saich, *From Rebel to Ruler: One Hundred Years of the Chinese Communist Party*, The Belknap Press of Harvard University Press, London (2021).

29. Kerry Brown, *The New Emperors: Power and Princelings in China*, I.B. Tauris & Co. Ltd, London (2014).
30. You Ji, Ed. Yongjin Zhang and Greg Austin, Power & Responsibility in Chinese Foreign Policy, Chapter: The PLA, CCP and formulation of China's Defence and Foreign Policy, Australian National University Press.
31. You Ji, 'Jiang Zemin's Command of the Military,' *The China Journal*, No. 45 (Jan 2001), University of Chicago Press for College of Asia and The Pacific, ANU pp. 131–138.
32. Mao Tse Tung, 'On the People's Democratic Dictatorship: In commemoration of the 28th anniversary of the Communist Party of China,' *Mao Tse-tung Selected Works* Vol. IV.
33. Zheng Wang, 'National Humiliation, History Education and the Politics of Historical Memory: Patriotic Education in China,' International Studies Quarterly, Vol. 52, No. 4 (December 2008), pp. 783–806.
34. Allen S. Whiting, 'Chinese Nationalism and Foreign Policy after Deng,' *The China Quarterly*, June 1995, No. 142, Cambridge University Press on behalf of SOAS, pp. 295–316.
35. David Shambaugh, 'The Dynamics of Elite Politics during the Jiang Era,' *The China Journal*, No. 45 (Jan 2001), University of Chicago Press on behalf of the College of Asia and the Pacific, ANU, pp. 101–111.
36. Richard McGregor, *The Party: The Secret World of China's Communist Rulers*, HarperCollins (2010).
37. ibid.
38. ibid.

Chapter 7: India and China: Attempt at Modus Vivendi

1. 'Brajesh Mishra & Mao's Smile,' *Frontline*, 28 February 2018.
2. Doc. 2304, Statement by Atal Bihari Vajpayee, Minister of External Affairs on arrival in Peking, 12 February 1979, in *India–China Relations 1947–2000: A Documentary Study*, Vol. 5, introduced and edited by A.S. Bhasin, Geetika Publishers, New Delhi 2018, p. 4849.

3. Nitin Gokhale, R.N. Kao, *Gentleman Spymaster*, Bloomsbury, New Delhi (2019), pp. 218–219.
4. S. Menon, 'Pacifying the Borders: The 1993 Border Peace & Tranquillity Agreement with China,' chapter in *Choices: Inside the Making of India's Foreign Policy*, Penguin Books (2016).
5. ibid.
6. Zheng Ruixiang, 'Shifting Obstacles in Sino-Indian Relations,' *The Pacific Review*, 6:1 (1993), pp. 63–70.
7. J. N. Dixit, *My South Block Years: Memoirs of a Foreign Secretary*, UBS Publishers' Distributors, New Delhi, January 1997, p. 24.
8. ibid., pp. 229–252.
9. Vijay Gokhale, 'The Road from Galwan: The Future of India–China Relations,' Carnegie India working paper, Carnegie Endowment for International Peace, 2021.
10. Excerpt, India–China Joint Press Communique issued on 23 December 1988.
11. Zhongguo Gongchandang Jianshe, Renmin Chubanshe, Zhonggongdang Chubanshe (History of the Chinese Communist Party), CCP Publication House (Beijing), February 2021.
12. Zheng Ruixiang, 'Shifting Obstacles in Sino-Indian Relations,' *The Pacific Review*, 6:1 (1993), pp. 63–70.
13. Memorandum between Government of India and Government of the People's Republic of China on the Resumption of Border Trade, 1 July 1992.
14. For a detailed rendition of events relating to the nuclear tests and its implications for India–China relations, see Chapter 3: 'Pokhran – How to Untie a Knot from the Tiger's Neck,' in *The Long Game: How the Chinese Negotiate with India*, Penguin Random House 2021.
15. S. Menon, 'Pacifying the Borders: The 1993 Border Peace & Tranquillity Agreement with China,' chapter in *Choices: Inside the Making of India's Foreign Policy*, Penguin Books (2016).
16. Shyam Saran, 'The India–China Border Dispute and After,' chapter in *How India Sees the World: Kautilya to the Twenty-First Century*, Juggernaut Books, pp. 123–148.

NOTES

17. Zhou claimed that the LAC was the 'so-called McMahon Line in the east and the line up to which each side exercises actual control in the West'. This assertion was accompanied by a small map that contained a series of disconnected points.
18. S. Menon, 'Pacifying the Borders: The 1993 Border Peace & Tranquillity Agreement with China,' chapter in *Choices: Inside the Making of India's Foreign Policy*, Penguin Books (2016).
19. ibid.
20. Article I of the Agreement on the Maintenance of Peace and Tranquillity Along the Line of Actual Control in the India–China Border Areas states, 'When necessary, the two sides shall jointly check and determine the segments of the line of actual control where they have different views as to its alignment.'
21. J. N. Dixit, *My South Block Years: Memoirs of a Foreign Secretary*, UBS Publishers' Distributors, New Delhi, January 1997, pp. 229–252.
22. Prime Minister Narasimha Rao Visits China, 6–9 September 1993, Publication of External Publicity Division, Ministry of External Affairs, New Delhi 10/1993.
23. Article X (1) of the said agreement.
24. General J.J. Singh, *The McMahon Line: A Century of Discord*, Harper Collins India (2019), pp 341.
25. ibid.
26. R.S. Kalha, *India–China's Boundary Issues: Quest for Settlement*, ICWA, Pentagon Press 2014. The author has identified the twelve areas of differences on page 215.
27. www.mea.gov.in.
28. For a detailed account of India–China negotiations on Sikkim, see Chapter 5: 'Half a Linguistic Pirouette,' *Long Game: How the Chinese Negotiate with India*, Penguin Random House, 2021.
29. Shyam Saran, 'The India–China Border Dispute and After,' *How India Sees the World: Kautilya to the Twenty-First Century*, Juggernaut Books, pp. 123–148.

30. S. Menon, 'Pacifying the Borders: The 1993 Border Peace & Tranquillity Agreement with China,' chapter in *Choices: Inside the Making of India's Foreign Policy*, Penguin Books (2016).
31. Nalin Surie, UGC Sponsored Conference on Sixty Years of India–China relations, Distinguished Lecture Series, Ministry of External Affairs, Thrissur, Kerala, 12 December 2011, www.mea.gov.in
32. Ashley Tellis, 'China and India in Asia,' chapter in Francine Frankel and Harry Harding (eds.), *The India–China Relationship: What the United States Needs to Know*, Carnegie Endowment for International Peace, September 2011.
33. Zheng Ruixiang, 'Shifting Obstacles in Sino-Indian Relations,' *The Pacific Review* 6Z:1, (1993), pp. 63–70.
34. Ashley Tellis, 'China and India in Asia,' chapter in Francine Frankel and Harry Harding (eds.), *The India–China Relationship: What the United States Needs to Know*, Carnegie Endowment for International Peace, September 2011.
35. Shyam Saran, 'The India–China Border Dispute and After,' *How India Sees the World: Kautilya to the Twenty-First Century*, Juggernaut Books (2017), pp. 123–148: 'The late Brajesh Mishra who was NSA to Vajpayee had once told me that the Chinese had informally indicated they would be prepared to settle for the return of about 10,000 sq kms of territory around the Tawang tracts including the Tawang settlement itself, in exchange for relinquishing the claim to the rest of Arunachal Pradesh. But I have not been able to find any corroboration of this.'
36. R.S. Kalha, *India–China's Boundary Issues: Quest for Settlement*, ICWA, Pentagon Press (2014), p. 225.

Chapter 8: Conclusions

1. F.W. Mote, 'The Yongzheng Emperor as Man and Ruler,' chapter in *Imperial China 900–1800*, Harvard University Press (1999).
2. Xiao Xiongyi, 'China's Foreign Policy in Transition: Understanding China's "Peaceful Development," *The Journal of East Asian Affairs*,

Vol. 19 No. 1 (Spring/Summer 2005), Institute for National Security Studies, pp. 74–112.
3. Zhang Wang, 'National Humiliation, History Education & the Politics of Historical Memory: Patriotic Education Campaign in China,' *International Studies Quarterly*, Vol. 52, No. 4 (December 2008), pp. 733–806.
4. Bonnie Glaser and Evan Medeiros, 'The Changing Ecology of Foreign Policy Making in Chinas: The Accession & Demise of the Theory of "Peaceful Rise",' *The China Quarterly*, No. 190 (June 2007), Cambridge University Press on behalf of SOAS, pp. 291–310.
5. James Mulvenon, 'Chairman Hu & the PLA's "New Historic Missions",' *China Leadership Monitor*, No. 27.
6. Barry Naughton, *The Chinese Economy: Transitions & Growth*, The MIT Press (2007).
7. Damien Ma, 'A Former Premier of China Speaks,' *The Atlantic*, 15 September 2011.
8. Yuen Yuen Ang, *China's Gilded Age: The Paradox of Economic Boom and Vast Corruption*, Cambridge University Press (2020).
9. James Mulvenon, To Get Rich in Unprofessional: Chinese Military Corruption in the Jiang Era.
10. Richard McGregor, *The Party: The Secret World of China's Communist Rulers*, HarperCollins 2010.
11. Elizabeth C. Economy, 'China's Imperial President: Xi Jinping Tightens his Grip,' *Foreign Affairs*, Vol. 93, No. 6 (Nov/Dec 2014), Council of Foreign Relations, pp. 80–91.
12. David Shambaugh, *China's Communist Party: Atrophy and Adaptation*, University of California Press, 2008.
13. Christopher Marsh, 'Learning from your Comrade's Mistakes: The Impact of the Soviet Past on China's Future,' *Communist & Post-Communist Studies*, Vol. 36, No. 3 (Sep 2003), University of California Press (2009), pp. 259–272.
14. Samson Yuen, 'Disciplining the Party: Xi Jinping's Anti-Corruption Campaign and Its Limits,' *China Perspectives*, 2014, No. 3 (99), French Center for Research on Contemporary China, pp. 41–47.

NOTES

15. In December 1929 the fledgling party held a meeting at Gutian, Fujian province at which it passed a resolution that entrenched the principle that the party had absolute leadership and full control over the Red Army (later re-named the PLA) and that it existed to serve the party's political objectives.
16. *Qiu Shi* magazine, No. 23, 1 December 2014.
17. Fatoumata Diallo, 'Xi Jinping and "Common Prosperity": New Governance Paradigm or Tool to Consolidate Power?,' *China Brief*, Vol. 21 Issue: 24, 17 December 2021, The Jamestown Foundation.

Index

Afghanistan–Pakistan issue, 163
African liberation movements, 78
agricultural taxes, 31
Al Qaeda affiliates, 99
American(s)
    containment strategy, 144
    diplomats, 57
    economic assistance, 75–76
    'exceptionalism,' 85
    hegemony, 156
    intervention in Iraq, 82
    oil company, 83
    relationship with India, 99
    strategy of 'peaceful evolution,' 49
    unilateralism, 85
American China Society, 54
American Embassy, 57
Anglo-Chinese war, 133
'anti-China' alliance, 162
anti-communist revolt, 5
anti-dumping activities, 134
anti-party, 37–38
anti-piracy missions off, 102
anti-reform, 16
Argentine light aircraft carrier, 89
Arunachal Pradesh, 145, 160
ASEAN+China Dialogue (1996), 85
ASEAN-China Free Trade Agreement, 74
ASEAN economies, 41
ASEAN Regional Forum (ARF), 72–73, 85

INDEX

Asian financial crisis, 73
'Asian NATO,' 108
Asia-Pacific Economic Conference, 85
Association of South-East Asian Nations (ASEAN), 41, 72–74, 85

Bab El-Mandeb, 109
Bangladesh, 162
banking system, 30–31
Bank of Communications, 31
Barshefsky, Charlene, 42–43
Beijing, 17, 48, 136–37
bilateral diplomacy in Africa, 85
'black swan' event, 73
blanket military sanctions, 105
blue-water capability, 101
border of tranquillity, 150
Border Peace and Tranquillity Agreement (BPTA), 150
border trade at Shipki La, 146
'bourgeois' liberalism, 12
Bo Xilai, 112–16, 123, 131, 171–73, 176
Bo Yibo, 2, 112–13
Brahmaputra river, 147, 159
BRICS (2006), 85
brutal repression, 59
Bulgaria, 51
Bush, George H.W., 53–54, 60

C4ISR, 102
capitalism, 11, 16, 117
capitalist experiment, 14
carrier-building program, 90–91
Central Asian Republics, 77, 163
Central Chinese Television, 103
Central Military Commission (CMC), 16–17, 101, 106, 171
century of humiliation, 59, 135, 169
'Change Through Trade,' 62
Chen Liangyu, 116, 123, 129
Chen Xitong, 116
Chen Yun, 2, 9–11, 116, 123
Chiang Kai-shek, 49, 133–34
China-Africa Development Fund, 81
China Agricultural Bank, 31
China Can Say No, 56–57
China/Chinese
  activism, 102
  America policy, 53
  anxieties, 82
  automobile market, 42
  communism, 132
  'continental' military tradition, 102
  'creeping expansionism,' 95
  diplomacy, 41, 75
  domestic market, 31
  economic landscape, 24
  economy, 124

encroachments, 94
European policy, 62–63
exceptionalism in Africa, 82
foreign policy, 48–49, 59, 156
GDP, 21
as 'great maritime power,' 101
independence and sovereignty, 53
industrialization process, 25
insecurities, 83
intellectuals and academics, 138
leadership, 4–5, 146
maritime scholars, 100
maritime strategy, 98
military publications, 100
modernization and reform, 126
Muslim population, 76
as Nanhai Zhudao, 91–92
national oil companies, 83
overlordship, 96–97
provincial leadership, 27
'socialist market economy,' 36
sovereign territory, 57–58
sovereignty and dignity, 56
trade surpluses, 46
urban landscape, 119
urban working class, 33
world's attention and admiration, 116
writings, 144–45
China Construction Bank, 31
China Democracy Forum, 137
China Development Bank, 123
China–Pakistan relationship, 145
China Petroleum and Chemical Corporation, 79
China's Territorial Seas, 92
'China Threat' narrative, 69
'China Threat' theory, 134, 169
China–US relations, 43–44
Chinese Academy of Social Sciences, 5
Chinese Communist Party, 2, 9, 12, 20, 22, 30, 59, 79, 112, 134, 166, 174–75
Chinese Empire, Strait of Malacca, 96–97
Chinese People's Liberation Army, 88
Chinese People's Political Consultative Committee, 136
'Chongqing Model,' 114
Clinton, William Jefferson, 53
'coddling dictators,' 54
commercial behaviour, 79
commercial decision-making powers, 30
Commission on Science, Technology, and Industry

for National Defence
(COSTIND), 101, 104
communism, 5, 12, 22, 49
communist parlance, 49
Communist Party of China, 36,
49, 56, 58–59, 65, 122
Communist Party of the Soviet
Union (CPSU), 8
Communist revolutionaries, 122
Communist rulers of Hungary,
5
Communist Youth League
faction, 128
'community of responsibility,' 62
Comprehensive Test Ban Treaty
(CTBT), 85
Confidence Building Measures
(CBM), 95
Confucius Institutes, 138
Congressional Research Service
(CRS) report, 72
constructive engagement policy,
60
constructive strategic
partnership, 55
Contiguous Zones, 91–92
Continental Shelf of PRC, 92
cradle-to-grave welfare-system,
132
CTBT negotiations, 162
cultural experimentation, 139

cultural or semi-religious
movements, 167
Cultural Revolution, 25, 129,
132
Cultural Revolution-like
movement, 2
currency undervaluation, 46
cyber-espionage, 105
Czechoslovakia, 51

Dai Bingguo, 153–54
Da Lac reef, 93
dan wei system, 32
decentralization, 25, 28
decision-making powers, 27, 31
Decision on Implementation
of Management System of
Taxes, 28
Declaration of Code of Conduct
(DOC), 94
Declaration of the Government
of the People's Republic of
China, 91–92
democratic elections, 54–55
Deng-ism, 37
Deng Liqun, 9–11, 14, 117
Deng Xiaoping, 2–3, 19, 51, 70,
111, 123, 143, 166
Dixit, J. N., 143, 150
dollar-diplomacy, 80
domestic economic
requirements, 41, 82

INDEX

domestic economy, 39

East Asia Summit (2005), 85
Eastern Han dynasty (25–200 CE), 92
Eastern NATO, 169
East Germany, 51
economic integration, 53
economic liberalization, 11, 15, 19–20
economic management, 24
economic policy, 24
economic reforms, 3, 8, 15, 18–19, 23, 37, 47, 116
'eight immortals', 113, 122–23
eroding socialism in China, 16
European capitals, 60
export-oriented production, 31

factionalism, 129
Fa Lun Gong, 137, 167
financial risk, 4
foreign capital, 25, 119
foreign direct investment (FDI), 25, 47
foreign exchange reform, 31
foreign invested enterprises (FIE), 25–26, 39
foreign investors, 27
Forum for China–Africa Cooperation (FOCAC), 80
freedom fighters, 78

Freedom of Navigation and Overflight Operation (FONOP), 58
Free Trade Agreement negotiations, 85
Free Trade Zone, 84
French companies, 90
'full employment' policy, 31

Gandhi, Rajiv, 141–45, 148
General Agreement on Trade and Tariffs (GATT), 40
German reunification, 61
global economic crises, 23
Global Financial Crisis, 46
global military alliance, 104
global trading system, 40
Gorbachev, Mikhail, 5, 142
Gorbachev's 'revisionist' policies, 9
Great Leap Forward (1958–62), 25, 134
Great Proletarian Cultural Revolution, 134
Greenspan, Alan, 42
guan xi, 122
Gu Kailai, 114–15
Gulf Cooperation Council, 84, 163
Guo Boxiong, 131

Hainan Island, 102–3

INDEX

Haksar, P.N., 143
Heywood, Neil, 114–15
Himachal Pradesh–Tibet Autonomous Region border, 146
Hong Kong, 15, 108
household contract responsibility system, 33
household registration system, 24, 34–35
Huang Ju, 128
Hu Jintao, 35, 39, 48, 57, 67–70, 77, 81, 83, 97–99, 101, 105–6, 111, 120–21, 125, 127–29, 131, 166, 168–69, 176, 178
Hungary, 4–5
Hu Yaobang, 11

ICBC, 31
ideological contamination, 9
'imperial families,' 122–23
'inactive plateau,' 153
India-China Border Areas, 150–51
India-China relationship, 143, 145
Indian Foreign Secretary, 143
Indian Ocean, 96, 100, 109
India–US partnership, 161–62
indigenous oil production, 82–83
Indo-Pacific region, 89

Indo-US partnership, 162
industrial modernization program, 33
inequalities in Chinese society, 172
intellectual justification, 138
intellectual property rights (IPR), 46, 64
international communism, 5
International Monetary Fund (IMF), 73
iron rice bowl, 22, 32, 132
Islamic radicalization in Afghanistan, 76

Jammu and Kashmir, 145
Japan, 21
Japan's Ogasawara-Guntō (Bonin) islands, 91
Jiang-Hu era, 132, 134–35, 139, 163–64, 167, 172
Jiang Zemin, 7, 12, 17–18, 29, 36, 40, 42, 48, 52–55, 57–58, 67, 69–70, 104–5, 111, 116, 118, 123, 125–28, 130, 134, 146, 150–51, 166, 168, 178
Jiang-Zhu era, 46–47
Jia Qinglin, 170
Ji Jianye, 123–24
Ji Shengde, 171
Joint Economic Group, 161

[212]

Joint Working Group (JWG), 143

KangQian Prosperous Era, 165
Kangxi (1661-1722), 165
Kinnaur district, 147
Kohl, Helmut, 61
Kravchuk, Leonid, 87
Kuznetsov-class aircraft, 87

labour mobility within China, 24
LAC. *See* Line of Actual Control (LAC)
Lama, Dalai, 63, 145, 156, 159
Lamy, Pascal, 44
landslide lake outburst flood (LLOF), 147
Law on Exclusive Economic Zone, 92
Law on Territorial Seas, 91–92
Lee Teng Hui, 54
Liaoning, 90
Liberation Daily, 12
liberation period, 22
Li Keqiang, 128
Line of Actual Control (LAC), 148, 151
   of 7 November 1959, 149, 151
   alignment, 152
   clarification episode, 153

Lin Youfang, 170
Li Peng, 9, 17, 29, 143, 146
Li Ruihuan, 2–3
Liu Huaqing, 89–91
Li Xiannian, 2, 116
Luo Yuan, 108–9

'Malacca Dilemma', 83, 169–70
'Malacca Strait Dilemma', 96–99
Maoism, 132
Maoist China, 118, 135
Maoist economics, 117
Mao Zedong, 49–50, 129, 141
maritime
   terrorism, 98–99
   voyages, 96
market economy, 85–86
market experimentation, 28
marketization, 36, 124
market-oriented economy, 36–37
market-oriented reforms, 11
market-preserving federalism, 27
mass 'patriotic education' campaign, 133
maximalist, 152
Medeiros, Evan, 67
medical insurance scheme, 33
Menon, Shivshankar, 142
Merkel, Angela, 61
Mishra, Brajesh, 141, 154

monopoly capitalist class, 132
Mt Namcha Barwa in Tibet, 147–48
Mukherjee, Pranab, 154, 159–60
multilateralism, 85
Mulvenon, James, 106–7
mutual delimitation, 95

Nagy, Imre, 5
Najibullah government in Afghanistan, 76
nationalism, 68–69, 133
nationalization of private enterprise, 132
National People's Congress, 18, 136
national rejuvenation, 133
National Security Advisor Brent Scowcroft, 60
Naval Review in Qingdao (April 2009), 103
neo-colonialism, 78
New York Stock Exchange, 54
Nixon, Richard, 10, 50
non-aggressive foreign policy, 51–52
non-performing assets (NPAs), 31
non-state-owned enterprises, 119
North Korea nuclearization, 168
Nuclear Suppliers Group, 158

Nyerere, Julius, 7

offshore defensive operations, 101
Oklahoma, 57–58
One-China policy, 159

Pakistan, 77, 145, 149–50, 156, 158, 161–62, 164
parliamentary democracy, 2
Party Central Economic Work Conference, 97–98
Party's Central Organization Department, 120
passive naval exchanges, 100
patriotic education campaign, 52, 133
patriotism, 59, 135
peaceful evolution, 11, 49–50
'peaceful rise,' 68
Peng Zhen, 2
pension scheme, 33
People's Armed Police (PAP), 125
people's democratic dictatorship, 132
People's Liberation Army (PLA), 14, 125
People's Republic of China, 67, 150–51, 153–54
Piech, Ferdinand, 62

Politburo Standing Committee (PBSC), 3, 9–10, 115, 129–31, 168, 170
political credibility, 46–47
political instability, 81–82
political reform, 8
political stability, 128
political tightening, 19–20
post-Cold War
  digital age, 139–40
  foreign policy, 52
  period, 65
  readjustment, 60
post-global financial crisis, 174
post-Tiananmen period, 119
Premier Zhu, 28
pre-revolutionary networks, 132
Princelings, 122
privatization, 29
pro-Mao nostalgia, 114
public housing scheme, 33
public image-making and diplomacy, 140
public ownership, 29
public sector reform, 28–29
Public Security Bureau (PSB), 125, 131

Qianlong (1735-1796), 165
Qing dynasty, 165
Qinghua University, 128
QUAD grouping, 108, 110

quasi-independent power centres, 131
quasi-monopolies, 120–21

RAND Corporation study, 84–85
Rao, P.V. Narasimha, 146, 150
rapid industrialization, 126
re-employment service centres, 32
reform-minded leadership, 10
regional hegemony, 111
Republican Party, 43
reunification, economic costs, 61
revenues sharing, 27–28
revisionism, 175
'revisionist' policies, 9
revolutionary groups, 78
Romania, 51
Roy, J. Stapleton., 53
Rubin, Robert, 43
rural migrant labour, 33
rural-to-urban migration, 24
rural-turned-urban workers, 34
Russia-India-China Group (2001), 85
Russian Federation, 76

Saudi-Iran relationship, 84
Schroeder, Gerhard, 61–62
Severino, Rodolfo, 75

INDEX

Shanghai, 108
Shanghai City, 23
Shanghai Cooperation Organization (SCO), 76, 85
'Shanghai Gang,' 128–29
Shenzhen, 14, 24, 108
Singh, Jaswant, 147–48
Singh, Manmohan, 154
Sino-American relations, 54
Sino-foreign joint ventures, 138
SINOPEC, 79
Sino-Russian relations, 65
Six Party Talks on Korea (2003), 85
Smith, Richard, 124
social instability, 28
socialism, 30
  in China, 176
  with Chinese characteristics, 132
socialist harmonious society, 35
socialist market economy, 18, 29, 36, 116–17, 132
social respectability, 127
social security systems, 32–33
social welfare, 23, 34
socio-economic benefits, 34
socio-economic principles, 36
Song dynasty (960-1279 CE), 92–93
Song Ping, 9
South China Sea, 58, 72, 91–93

Southeast Asian kingdoms, 96–97
southern tour, 16–17, 21
'South Tibet,' 160
Soviet collapse, 174
Soviet Communism, 13, 118
Soviet Communist Party, 49, 175
Soviet-era carriers, 90
Sperling, Gene, 43
spiritual movements, 137
state capitalism, 117
state-of-the-art foreign technology, 104–5
State-owned Assets Supervision and Administration Commission (SASAC), 120–21
state-owned Chinese oil companies, 78
State-Owned Enterprises (SOEs), 25, 29, 47, 118
  conglomerates, 123
  Party supervision over, 137
  privatization, 120
  State's control, 120
state-run China Railway group, 123
Steinmeier, F. W., 62
Stockholm International Peace Research Institute (SIPRI), 81, 88

INDEX

Strait of Hormuz, 109
Straits of Malacca, 96
strategic oil partnership, 82
'string of pearls,' 100–101
'striving for achievement,' 177
Sumdorong Chu Valley, 142, 151
Sutlej rivers, 159

Taiwan Straits, 94
Tanzania-Zambia railway, 78
taxation
   and budget reforms, 32
   and investment policies, 26
tax-revenue sharing, 28
Tiananmen Incident, 7, 22, 56, 115–16, 166, 172–73
Tiananmen Massacre, 59
Tiananmen Square, 137
Tibet's Party Secretary (1988-1992), 166–67
tormentors, 64–65
trade negotiators, 42
trans-national corporations, 137
Trudeau, Pierre, 10
Tsung-Dao Lee, 6–7, 50
tuan pai, 128

unemployment insurance guarantee, 32
UNOCAL, 83
UN Security Council, 158
unspecified market liberalization, 63
urbanization, 35, 126
urban residents, 34
US-China Economic and Security Commission in 2009, 106
US-China face off, 56
US Federal Reserve Board, 30–31, 42
US Navy EP-3 surveillance aircraft, 58
US Quadrennial Defence Review 2006, 108
US Treasury securities, 46

Vajpayee, Atal Bihari, 141–42, 153, 161–62
Varyag, 88
Venkataraman, R., 146
victimization, 52, 133
Vogel, Ezra, 9–10

Walesa, Lech, 4–5
Wang Zhen, 2, 9, 123
War on Terror, 74–75
welfare-state system, 117
Wen Jiabao, 31, 35, 47, 68, 79, 123, 128, 153–54
western business conglomerates, 137
Western capitalism, 16

western commercial interests in Africa, 82
Western-style democracy in China, 2
western-style governance, 136
World Economic Forum at Davos, 68
World Trade Organization (WTO), 40, 55
Wu Bangguo, 128
Wu Shengli, 103

Xi Jinping, 2, 111–12, 123, 166, 170, 173, 177–78
Xinjiang Uyghur Autonomous Region, 66, 76
Xi Zhongxun, 23
Xu Caihou, 131
Xu Qinxian, 129

Yang Baibing, 17, 130
Yang Jiechi, 159–60
Yang Shangkun, 2, 14, 17, 130
Yao Yilin, 9

Yarlung Tsangpo, 147
Yeltsin, Boris, 12, 65–66
Ye Xuanping, 123
Yin Zhuo, 101
Yong Le, 96
Yongzheng, 165–66
Yuanhua corruption scandal, 170–72
Yuen Ang, 124

Zeng Qinghong, 128
Zhang Yu, 101
Zhao Ziyang, 2, 4–6, 11, 23, 143
Zheng Bijian, 83
Zheng He, 96
Zhongnanhai, 122
Zhou Enlai, 148
Zhou Yongkang, 131, 176
zhuangda fangxiao, 118–19
Zhu Rongji, 12–13, 17, 23, 25–26, 29, 31, 33, 36–38, 41, 43, 117–18, 123, 147–48, 170
'*zou chu qu*' policy, 79

About the Author

Vijay Keshav Gokhale (b. 1959) spent nearly four decades in the Indian Foreign Service. He served as India's High Commissioner to Malaysia and Ambassador to Germany and to the People's Republic of China, and retired as the Foreign Secretary in January 2020. He worked on matters relating to China for a significant portion of his diplomatic career. His assignments in Hong Kong, Taipei and Beijing between 1982 and 2017, and his postings in New Delhi at various levels, have given him insights into Chinese politics.

Gokhale was present in China during the 1989 Tiananmen Square incident and witnessed many of the happenings. He regards the incident as a seminal event in modern Chinese politics, which ought to be studied for a deeper understanding of China. He currently lives in Pune with his wife Vandana, and devotes his time to the study of China.

He is the author of *Tiananmen Square: The Making of a Protest* (HarperCollins, 2021) and *The Long Game: How the Chinese Negotiate with India* (Penguin, 2021).